Fundamentals of Riding

Fundamentals of Riding

LEARNING THE ESSENTIAL SKILLS

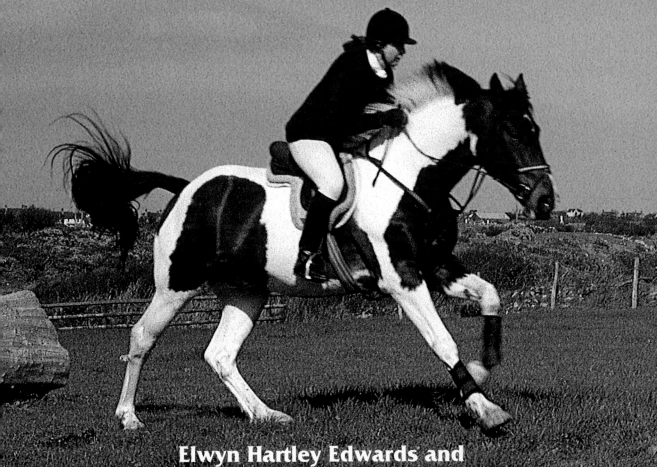

**Elwyn Hartley Edwards and
Sian Thomas** BHSI

Copyright © 1998 Elwyn Hartley Edwards and Sian Thomas

First published in the UK in 1998
by Swan Hill Press, an imprint of Airlife Publishing Ltd

British Library Cataloguing-in-Publication Data
  A catalogue record for this book
  is available from the British Library

ISBN 1 85310 852 9

Typeset by Phoenix Typesetting, Ilkley, West Yorkshire.
Printed in Hong Kong

Swan Hill Press
an imprint of Airlife Publishing Ltd
101 Longden Road, Shrewsbury, SY3 9EB, England

Contents

Acknowledgements

The authors wish to record their thanks to:
Helen Jones of the Gors-Wen Riding School, Anglesey, who allowed us to use the stallion Spring Warrior, and to Catrin Plews of Brackendine Stud, Anglesey, who rode her stallion Picasso over the cross-country fences; Nichola Hughes for demonstrating the gymnastic exercises for the chapter 'Fit to Ride' and Caroline Young for riding the exercises on the lunge.

We are also indebted to Sian's parents, Mr and Mrs W. E. Thomas, proprietors of the Snowdonia Riding Stables, for the use of their facilities and to the staff of the Snowdonia Stables for their assistance.

Finally, we wish to express our gratitude to Julie Thomas who collated the manuscript with such care and to Leslie Lane who took many of the photographs.

Introduction

A fundamental Principle of War is the establishment of a clear progression of objectives, a matter that is just as relevant when it comes to the writing of instructional books on riding, or, indeed, any other subject.

Following that precept, this book is written and illustrated with the amateur one-horse owner/rider very much in mind. Its principal purpose is to help him or her (and it is more likely to be her than otherwise) to master the *basic* skills which lead to more effective and enjoyable riding for *both* members of the partnership. All else being equal, the improved level of performance will allow the pair to compete creditably in a variety of events at, or perhaps beyond, a good local level.

Not for a moment would we suggest that you can learn to ride effectively with the reins in one hand and a book in the other. Nonetheless, the book has an important role to play and can act as an invaluable supplement to lessons given by qualified and competent instructors with necessarily limited time at their disposal.

The authors. Sian Thomas on the Irish Sport Horse, Dr Dolittle (Paddy) and Elwyn Hartley Edwards who is riding Marcus, the Hungarian Nonius.

It serves to provide the indispensable guidelines; it fills the inevitable gaps and helps to clarify and fix the details of technique. Very importantly, the book is able to enlarge on the theory underpinning the rational movements and practice of correct, and successful, riding and so contributes significantly to a wider, deeper understanding of the whole.

(Obviously, one cannot ride on the basis of theory alone, but it is very necessary for riders to know what they are attempting to interpret from the saddle and why the movement or whatever should be considered desirable or even necessary. Of

Taurus, bred by the Dwyfor Stud by the Thoroughbred El Cid out of a Welsh Cob mare.

course, there are the 'naturals' who apply, unconsciously, their rare genius to obtain results with seemingly minimal effort – but there are very, very few of them!)

The majority of amateur riders, most of whom have responsibilities other than with their association with horses – jobs, homes to run, studies and so on – do, in our experience, appreciate that they need a modicum of professional instruction. They recognise that it will improve the performance of themselves and their horses and so will increase the pleasure that both obtain from the exercise.

(Opposite Above):
Marcus, a Warmblood of Hungarian Nonius breeding and an eminently 'rideable' sort.

(Opposite Below):
Spring Warrior (Winston) a 17h stallion by the supreme Cleveland Bay champion Forest Saga out of Spring Value, a Thoroughbred mare with lines to Pall Mall and to the Derby winners Crepello and Ocean Swell. The stallion stands at Helen Jones's Gors-Wen School, Anglesey.

For many, however, circumstances do not always allow instructional sessions to be as frequent as they would like or, indeed, as they may need to be, and for them the book becomes an essential back-up if progress is to be maintained. Indeed, it is probably true to say that the value of the book increases in direct ratio to the infrequency of the lessons.

For the illustrations we have selected horses to demonstrate the school movements and exercises that would be within the reach of the amateur rider aspiring to take part in club level competition at a good medium standard. They were not expensive horses, initially, and they are all manageable by the one-horse owner who has other responsibilities to consider.

One of the horses is a Thoroughbred/Welsh Cob cross. He is a talented horse approaching advanced movements in his work, but was not an expensive acquisition. Another is the Irish half-bred (sports horse) – again, the type of good all-round horse affordable by the one-horse owner. Marcus, the Hungarian Nonius, is an example of the European Warmblood, now becoming increasingly popular throughout the world. He is an eminently 'rideable' horse and well suited on that account to the rider who has limited time to devote to his schooling.

Spring Warrior, 'Winston', the Cleveland Bay/Thoroughbred stallion, is the exception. He is representative of a particularly

Paddy, a very good example of the Irish Sport Horse which relies principally on the Thoroughbred and the Irish Draught cross.

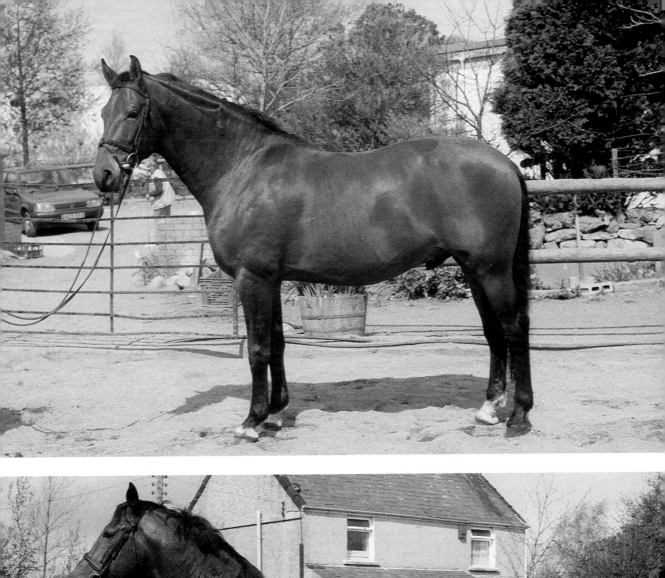
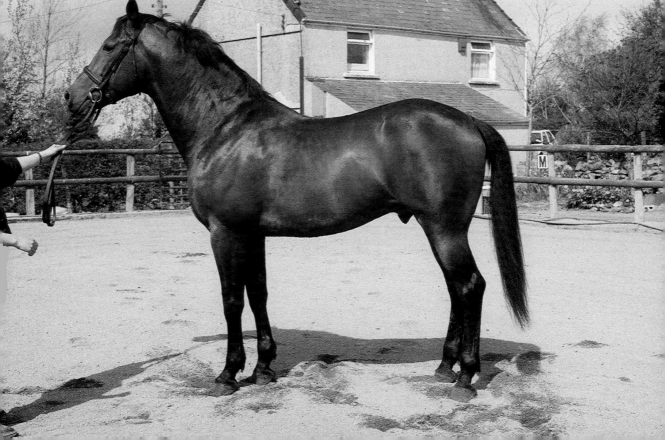

good cross, as good as and probably better than most in Europe, if not always sufficiently appreciated. He is not by any means beyond the capacity of the club rider, but it became evident during his training that he had the potential to be an outstanding performer.

All these horses were trained by Sian Thomas in the progressive system of schooling movements described in this book.

(Left):
The Brackendine Stud's coloured stallion, of predominantly Irish ancestry and owing much to the Irish Draught. He, too, stands on Anglesey.

The coloured stallion used to illustrate the cross-country chapter is another product of correct basic training. He is owned by the Brackendine Stud, Anglesey, and, although entire, is the sort of manageable horse suited to the amateur.

For convenience, and in the interests of a logical progression, the book is divided into a number of sections.

Considerable emphasis is given initially to the sub-divisions

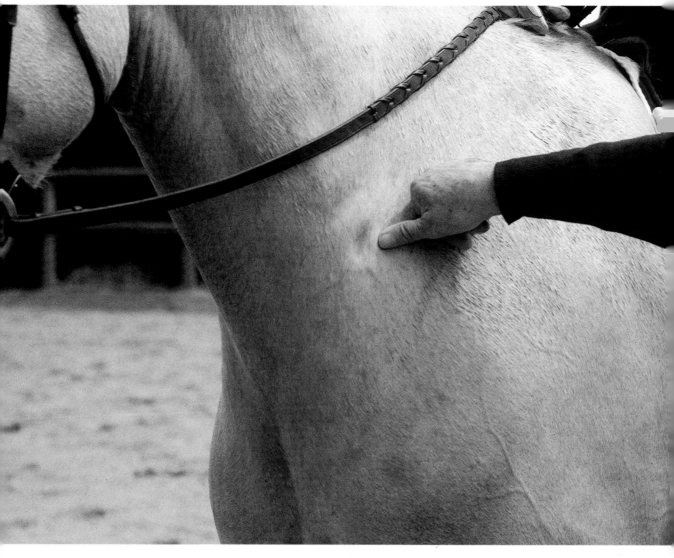

This depression in Taurus's neck is known as the Prophet's Thumbmark. Legend has it that the Prophet Mohammed placed his hand in blessing on the necks of five superlative mares, the founders of the principal Arab Horse families. It is said that the mark is carried to this day by the very best of their descendants.

and correctness of the three paces, and the transitions from one to another.

This is followed by the school figures, or exercises, designed to achieve a correct build-up of muscles and to supple the horse. Thereafter the more advanced movements, described in text, photographs and supporting diagrams, are those which result in an increasingly correct outline leading to an immeasurably enhanced balance.

Using the basis of the essential work on the flat there are the jumping chapters, containing a variety of training exercises that begin with the simple pole grids and go on to the jumping of substantial fences.

However, the most important section is the first which concentrates initially on the seat and the correct (the most effective) application of the aids. It is the most important because it is upon the correctness of the rider's seat, when the bodyweight is carried always in supple balance with the movement, that the success of all subsequent work depends.

The seat described and illustrated is that practised at the established classical schools of Europe. It has been proved to be the most effective, and the principles practised and established on the flat can be adapted to provide the basis for both arena and cross-country jumping.

However, saddles play a large part in helping the rider to acquire a practical, 'classical' seat. Encouragingly, there is now, more than ever, an awareness of the saddle's influence on the rider's effective position and the freedom of the horse's movement, and so we have included in the first section an examination of the saddle and its fitting, as well as studying the bridling arrangements.

Then, of course, there has to be consideration of the human factor – we cannot expect the horse to do everything for us. Communication between rider and horse is achieved in three parts: there is the physical contact through the aids given by leg, hand and bodyweight; the mental influence projected by the rider; and then, which is the most difficult of all, the rider's ability to listen to the horse's response through both mind and body. Only when that is possible do we have communication in the partnership between two sentient beings. Up to that point the rider is not so much communicating with the horse as dominating him. By doing so a limitation is imposed on the success of the partnership.

In time, the intelligent rider will develop the receptive sensitivity that allows riding with the mind as well as the body, but there is no hope of that being accomplished until such time as the rider is in unconscious physical harmony with the horse.

In consequence, just as we work to improve the physical and gymnastic conditioning of the horse, so we must ensure that the rider has a commensurate standard of fitness. For that reason part of the first section is devoted to suppling, strengthening and postural exercises for the rider; a matter of a fit rider on a fit horse – anything else is doomed to failure.

Over 60 years ago one of the world's great horsemen, Henry Wynmalen, a Dutchman by birth, who expressed himself in the English language better than most Englishmen, wrote the book *Equitation* (Country Life).

It was introduced by his friend, the late Colonel V.D.S. ('Pudding') Williams, a man who gave great encouragement to the growth of dressage in Britain and exerted a profound influence on the then fledgling sport of horse trials. 'Pudding'

Williams concluded his foreword to *Equitation* with these words:

> 'Good riding is an affair of skill, but bad riding is an affair of courage.
>
> Good riding will last through age, sickness and decrepitude, but bad riding will last only as long as youth, health and strength supply courage.'

Unreservedly, the elder author of this book affirms the truth of those assertions.

A paragraph previously in his foreword, Colonel Williams had written:

> 'You cannot learn to ride from a book alone, but here is one from which you can learn much of the Art of Equitation.'

We would not presume to regard this book as nearly approaching Wynmalen's lucid treatise but we hope it will help riders to understand and practise a *little* of the Art.

Elwyn Hartley Edwards
Sian Thomas BHSI

Section 1

Chapter 1

The Seat

In an age when political correctness was not a consideration, Miguel de Cervantes (1547–1616), the author of *Don Quixote*, wrote that 'the seat on a horse makes gentlemen of some and grooms of others'. In our modern climate and in the context of this book the epigram might better be paraphrased to read: 'The seat on a horse makes riders of some and passengers of others.'

The posture adopted by the rider, which, for convenience, generations of horsemen have referred to as 'the seat', is fundamental to successful and enjoyable riding. It is on the seat adopted by the rider that the free, unrestricted movement of the horse depends. Quite simply, if the rider is out of balance then so is the horse. Furthermore, it is the seat which allows or inhibits the effective application of the aids (signals) given by the legs, the hands, the trunk, back and so on – and which form the means of communication on a physical plane. It follows, incontrovertibly, that the dialogue will be impaired in direct ratio to the postural failings of the rider.

The theory of the *effective* seat is not new, nor is it difficult to understand. Essentially, it is straightforward enough, although it is less easily put into practice. Where confusion arises it is often due to a misunderstanding of basic principles or, perhaps, in some instances, being unaware of their existence.

In recent years we have heard a lot about the 'classical' seat, sometimes, alas, propounded by self-appointed experts who are without the formal, recognised qualifications based on a sound, all-round training progression. There are, of course, a number of skilled riders and good teachers who have no need of formal qualifications. Indeed, we need look no further than some of the gifted Portuguese and Spanish riders, but inevitably there are the 'false prophets' who detract from the laudable objectives of the more experienced and can contribute to an unnecessary muddying of the equestrian waters.

In itself, the *word* 'classical' is open to differences of interpretation, but the etymology is really not important. The seat has to be *effective*, and if that is synonymous with 'classical', so be it. Thankfully, there is substantial agreement on what constitutes an effective seat for flatwork riding. Obviously, it requires adaptation for riding over fences but the principles remain the same. The keyword is balance, to which may be added the adjective 'fluid'.

As a general definition of the effective/classical seat, it is that in which the bodyweight, by virtue of an erect trunk, flexible hips and a supple back, conforms softly to the movement and remains in balance with it at all the paces. It is independent of the reins for its security and allows freedom of movement to the body's component parts in 'managing and directing the powers of the horse'.

It all began 2,000 years ago with the Greek general, historian, philosopher and agriculturalist, Xenophon (c430–356BC). He described the seat of a man on a horse 'not as though he were sitting on a chair but rather as though he were standing upright with his feet apart', to which can be added 'and with the knees bent'.

Over 2,000 years later, horsemen enjoying the benefits of the saddle and stirrup, neither of which were known in Xenophon's classical Greek civilisation, are saying much the same thing.

Foremost among the reforming cavalry gurus of the nineteenth century were men of the calibre of Louis Nolan, who was killed in the ill-fated charge of the Light Brigade at Balaclava, and Francis Dwyer, an Anglo-Irishman employed in the Imperial Austrian cavalry.

Nolan was responsible for the Army UP saddle, which is still in use, whilst Dwyer pioneered the use of the Hungarian light cavalry saddle. He did so in the firm belief that it allowed the rider's weight to be positioned over the fourteenth dorsal vertebra. He called it, with every justification, 'the keystone of the arch' for it is the only vertebra that stands upright, the first 13 from the point of the neck's attachment are inclined *backwards*, while vertebrae 15–18 and the six lumbar vertebrae incline *forwards*. He argued, and he was right, that the fourteenth vertebra represented 'the centre of movement' and he summarised as a general rule: 'The saddle in the centre of the horse's back, the girths, stirrups and rider in the centre of the saddle.'

In our own time, the late Colonel Hans Handler, who succeeded Colonel Alois Podhajsky as Director of Vienna's Spanish Riding School, gave this definition of the seat:

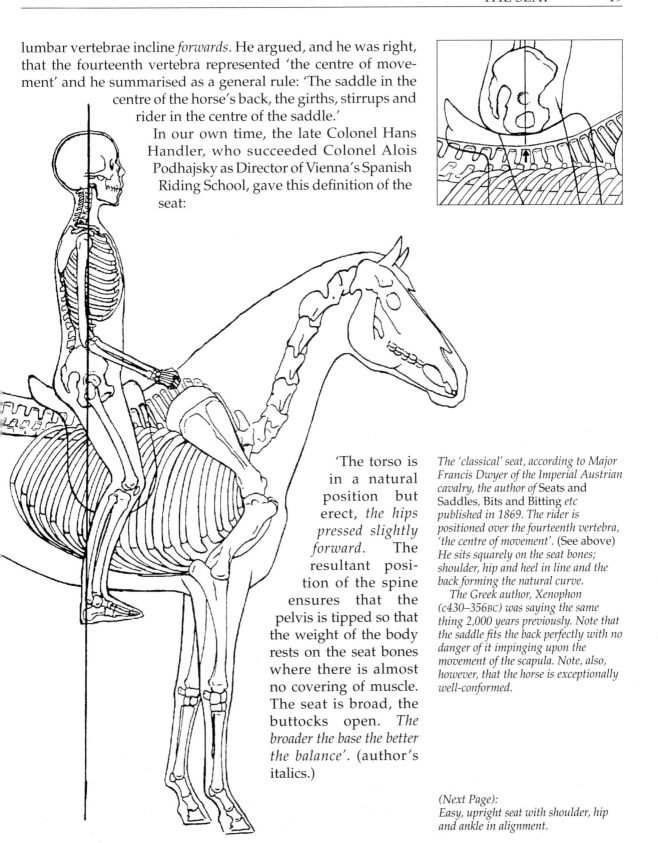

'The torso is in a natural position but erect, *the hips pressed slightly forward*. The resultant position of the spine ensures that the pelvis is tipped so that the weight of the body rests on the seat bones where there is almost no covering of muscle. The seat is broad, the buttocks open. *The broader the base the better the balance*'. (author's italics.)

The 'classical' seat, according to Major Francis Dwyer of the Imperial Austrian cavalry, the author of Seats and Saddles, Bits and Bitting *etc* published in 1869. The rider is positioned over the fourteenth vertebra, 'the centre of movement'. (See above) He sits squarely on the seat bones; shoulder, hip and heel in line and the back forming the natural curve.

The Greek author, Xenophon (c430–356BC) was saying the same thing 2,000 years previously. Note that the saddle fits the back perfectly with no danger of it impinging upon the movement of the scapula. Note, also, however, that the horse is exceptionally well-conformed.

(Next Page):
Easy, upright seat with shoulder, hip and ankle in alignment.

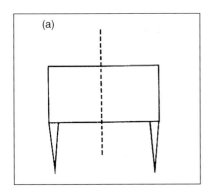

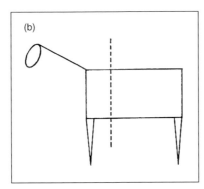

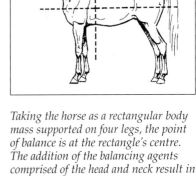

To comply with the requirement for the position of the pelvis, then the shoulder, hip and heel should form one straight line which is balanced by the straight line connecting elbow, hand and horse's mouth. Such a seat permits the back to be held in its natural curve. Used in conjunction with the hand and leg it is then possible, after much application, to exert a powerful, driving influence on the horse. (Interestingly, some riders of the German and Scandinavian school depart from what might be considered the classical position exemplified by the Spanish School, France's Saumur and the Iberian horsemen by tilting the pelvis backwards through as much as 20° to produce a driving aid of great power that is, nonetheless, literally behind the movement. This forceful driving-from-the-back-seat position is ugly but is clearly very effective when practised by experts – but it suits only the most strongly built horses.)

Of course, definitions and descriptions of the ideal seat amount to little or nothing unless one first appreciates what is meant by riding 'in balance' and 'with the movement', and that entails an elementary knowledge of the horse's balance.

Quite simply, the centre of gravity of the horse, or the centre of balance, if you prefer, is in the middle of the animal's body at the point of intersection of two imaginary lines. The first of them is drawn vertically to the ground from just behind the withers, whilst the second is taken horizontally from the point of the shoulder to the rear.

This is the position of the centre of balance at a square halt with the head and neck held naturally and it does not alter materially at the ordinary school paces unless the horse is carrying his weight over the forehand to an unusual degree. However, when the horse is moving at speed with the head and neck extended, or at the moment when taking off at a fence, the point moves forward. Conversely, in the state of collection, when the neck is carried high with the face in the vertical plane, and the hindlegs are shortening the base by being strongly engaged under the body and with the quarters lowered in consequence,

Taking the horse as a rectangular body mass supported on four legs, the point of balance is at the rectangle's centre. The addition of the balancing agents comprised of the head and neck result in the point moving forward (b). In the horse at halt with head and neck carried normally the centre of balance has been fixed at the intersection of the vertical and horizontal lines and in the centre of the body (c).

Detail of the seat, balanced, classical or what you will, but essentially practical.

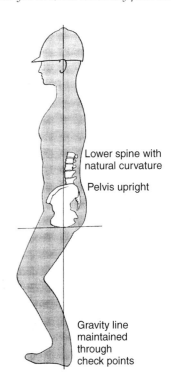

Lower spine with natural curvature

Pelvis upright

Gravity line maintained through check points

then the point of balance shifts at least a little towards the rear. When the horse turns or moves laterally the centre of balance is shifted to the side in the direction of the movement.

It can be seen that the head and neck, corresponding to a sort of pendulum, are, in fact, used as a balancing agent. When crossing broken ground, for instance, they are raised and lowered to effect the constant adjustments to the balance made necessary by the going.

The rider is in balance with the horse when his bodyweight is carried lightly over the centre of the horse's balance, where it causes the least possible interference to the movement. The rider is out of balance when his weight is carried in front of or behind the centre of balance. In the first instance the horse's forehand is overloaded, in the second the quarters, the engine of the horse, are compelled to operate whilst carrying some portion of the rider's weight. In both cases the freedom of movement is restricted. Similarly, in the turns and lateral work the bodyweight must generally accord with the shift of the centre of balance to the inside. (In practice, this is accomplished by the rider weighting the inside seat bone by pressing down into the corresponding stirrup iron. Additionally, in making changes of direction, the shoulders and hips must correspond by being in alignment with those of the horse. For instance, in turning to the right the rider's head will be inclined in the same direction. As a result the left shoulder and left hip will be slightly in advance, both then being parallel to the shoulders and hips of the horse and thus conforming to the movement.)

To bring the point home, experiment by carrying a child on your shoulders. So long as the child remains still and upright, with his centre of gravity in line with your own, walking, or even running, is not difficult. Problems occur when the child bends forward or throws his weight backwards. If he swings backwards *and* forwards it is almost impossible to move at all. (Imagine the stress caused to the horse galloping over undulating, broken ground with a novice on his back!)

(*Note.* To appreciate the positioning of the head and neck in their role as a balancing agent it is useful to study these figures, which are taken from the work done at the turn of the century by the French veterinarians Bourgelat and Duhousset.

A horse weighing 348kg (767lb) standing square with the head held normally carries 190kg (419lb) on the forehand and 158kg (348lb) on the hindlegs, a difference of 32kg (71lb). If the neck is *lowered*, the forehand carries 243kg (536lb) and the quarters carry 108kg (238lb), a difference of 135kg (298lb). When the neck is *raised*, 181kg (400lb) is placed over the forehand and 167kg (368lb) over the quarters, a difference of only 14kg (32lb). It will be seen that the horse becomes lighter in front (and lighter

(Far Left):
Hands suitable for driving a tram, wrist and forearm stiff, no sensitivity in the fingers.

(Left):
The hands properly held. The line from shoulder through to fingers is soft and relaxed.

in the hand) when the weight carried by the quarters is increased.

The effect that the rider has on the weight distribution is as follows. A rider of 58kg (128lb) sitting over the centre of balance places 37kg (82lb) on the forehand and 21kg (46lb) on the hindlegs. If the rider inclines the body to the rear 46kg (101lb) of the weight is carried on the hindlegs.

Colonel Handler's succinct definition of the rider's seat is admirable and entirely sufficient for his peers, but for the less advanced rider some expansion is needed.

Starting at the top we have to consider the head, the weight of which is out of all proportion to the rest of the body. In consequence its influence on the rider's overall posture is critical. It should be held erect, but not stiffly, on top of the shoulders. If it is allowed to tip forward, a common failing even in advanced riders, the trunk becomes out of balance in all of its components, exerting a locking effect as far down as the ankle.

The chest must be open but not thrust outwards, pigeon fashion, so that the back assumes an exaggerated curve. If that is allowed to happen the weight will be pushed on the front of the seat bones and the rider's bottom will be pushed out inelegantly behind. If the chest droops, in conjunction with the leg held in front of the vertical line, the rider sits on the tail on the back of the seat bones and is behind the movement, out of balance and entirely ineffectual.

The desirable position of the leg; the seat is broad, the trunk resting on the seat bones.

The ideal posture seen from the rear. The trunk is upright, shoulders straight in line with the horse's hips and the legs lie unobtrusively in light contact.

The position viewed from the front.

The position maintained at the walk, the rider sitting over the seat bones with the trunk upright.

The position at walk seen from directly in front. The movement and position of the horse is exemplary.

(Far left and left)
Two examples of the rider sitting with a 'collapsed' hip and therefore out of balance.

Leg drawn back with the rider perched on the fork and without contact through the seat bones.

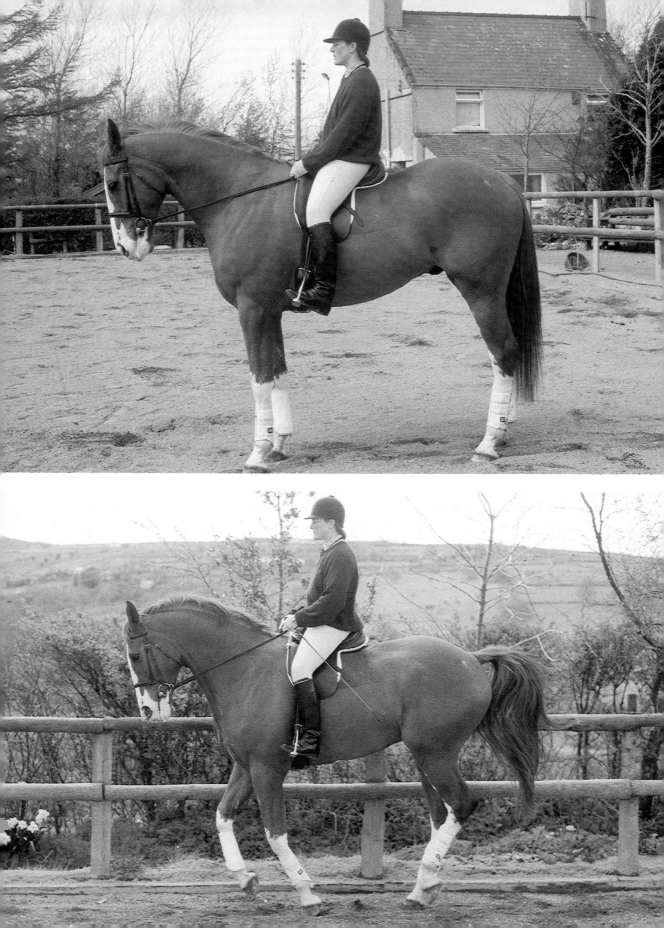

Now to the arm, which is held naturally to the side but never clamped to the body. The hand, following the line of the forearm, is very slightly curved, with the thumb held uppermost over the index finger. The hands are held the width of the bit apart, the thumb of the right hand pointing towards the base of the horse's left ear and vice versa. Hands clasped together and tucked back into the stomach are useless since they create a block at that point preventing the movement created in the quarters from passing through the whole horse. Hands 'broken' at the wrist are equally ineffectual, whilst those held with backs uppermost as though on the handlebars of a bicycle are an abomination. Such a position causes the muscles of the forearm to be tensed and thus the hands and fingers become inflexible and insensitive.

Central to the riding position, as well as to the human body, are the hips, which *lead* the movement. They are pushed a little forward giving the impression of the stomach being pushed upwards and forwards towards the horse's ears. Always they must be flexible. If they lock, which is the common fault, the back loses its ability to absorb the movement through oscillation.

The position of the leg and the length of stirrup is just as critical. After all, the leg is the principal agent of communication.

Initially, therefore, the rider, while sitting centrally, has to extend the leg downwards and then, remembering that the horse is to all intents barrel-shaped, to *wrap* the leg lightly around the frame. That action, of course, precludes entirely any inward, gripping pressure from the knee which would only serve to raise the seat out of the saddle rather than to deepen it. Furthermore, any effort to grip with the knee locks that joint and restricts the use of the lower leg.

Security is maintained through the contact of the upper thigh. The inside of the knee rests against the saddle without gripping it and always needs to be pointed. If it straightens the whole limb is stiffened and that effect is passed upwards to the trunk.

The relaxed lower leg is held *lightly* on the horse's side. Ideally one should aim to feel the horse *breathe* through the leg, responding to the movement of the horse's flank by remaining entirely supple. NEVER, EVER SHOULD THE LOWER LEG GRIP. If it does the knee comes away from the saddle and the contact of the thigh is reduced, whilst the horse, poor chap, becomes confused by the constant pressure. As a rule of thumb, to arrive at the practical length of leather, the tread of the stirrup iron should be on a level with the ankle.

The foot when in position should be nearly parallel to the ground but with the weight more in the heel than otherwise and the toe pointing to the front. Do not, however, *push* the heel

(Opposite Above):
Leg forward, waist collapsed. Politely, the horse pretends he has not noticed.

(Opposite Below):
The seat at the departure into canter, body upright, leg correctly placed in applying the aid.

down, since this will only tense and stiffen the calf. Instead, think of gently *raising* the toe, which is a different thing altogether, and using the stirrup as a 'foot rest'. The stirrup is held on the ball of the foot and will stay in place more easily if the inside of the foot is a shade lower that the outside. This position will also ensure that the knee continues to lie lightly in contact with the saddle.

To conform with the shoulder-hip-heel-in-a-straight-line principle the lower leg will be drawn *slightly* to the rear, but do not allow the leg to be carried too far back since that will limit its effective application for work on the flat.

To re-iterate the basic rules:

- The head, held erect, rests squarely on the shoulders; the shoulders on top of the hips, the upper body is held over the foot.
- Shoulders and hips are aligned with those of the horse.
- The waist and so the small of the back provide the supple connection between the upper and lower body. It absorbs and follows the movement by reason of its flexibility.

Chapter 2

The System of Communication

Communication with the horse is made through the medium of the mind, the voice and a system of signals made by the legs, the hands, the back and seat and the disposition of the bodyweight. Occasionally, the whip and spur act to support, or reinforce, the physical actions.

The physical aids, as the best manuals will tell you, are termed 'natural', whilst the whip and spur (and often, surprisingly, the voice) are termed 'artificial'. Their purpose is to reinforce, as necessary, the 'natural' aids, particularly their driving capacity, and they have an important role to play in fine tuning the physical aid to the point where its lightest application is rewarded with an immediate response from the horse in what amounts to a conditioned reflex.

The aids, the corporate title accorded to these signals at some point in the equestrian development, are the means through which the rider makes requests of the horse and influences the latter's movement and posture. They are, if you like, the language of riding.

To all intents, the aids are inter-dependent, acting in concert and not in isolation. They operate in the sequence prepare–act–yield and, on occasions, they are employed to resist unwanted movements.

The preparatory aids are employed to secure the horse's attention and correct the balance before aids are applied asking for a specific movement. For instance, when moving off from halt into walk, the horse's attention is attracted by a light squeeze of the legs followed, almost simultaneously, by the closing of the fingers in another gentle squeeze. The horse is then ready to respond to the acting aid which asks for the move off into walk.

The aids yield the moment a response is obtained and ideally a split second before that point, the discontinued pressures telling the horse that he has done what was wanted. The whole business of riding, indeed, the essence of *chivalry*, a word derived from the French *cheval* (horse), is about good manners. We should not demand that the horse do this or do that, but rather we should remember our manners and say 'please' and 'thank-you'. Not surprisingly, it works better that way.

Finally, the aids may resist to combat an evasive action on the part of the horse. The hands, for instance, can *resist* to restrain an impetuous forward movement, or one leg may be used to discourage an unwanted shift of the quarters in one direction or another.

The word 'aids', as a description of the system of the physical signals of communication, was coined fairly late in equestrian history. Horsemen of the Renaissance and those of the following seventeenth and eighteenth centuries, the very age of 'classicism', talked and wrote about the 'helps'. It means much the same thing but *help* has, perhaps, a more attractive nuance than the somewhat clinical, and perhaps authoritarian, *aid* and is the more expressive word.

Often disregarded, but integral to the system of signals is the first link in the chain, the head. I term it the first link because, apart from its initiation of the physical movement, actions taken without due and prior consideration are likely to prove abortive. It *is* necessary to think ahead, to organise the horse before attempting the movement, and to do so the engagement of the head, or rather its content, is an absolute essential.

In this sense the head is being regarded simplistically and not in relation to the enormously important *influence of the mind*. To be able to communicate with the horse on a mental plane is an acquired art and no specific instructions are available that will lead to its attainment. It is a matter of awareness, of sensitivity, concentration, projection and receptivity. Once we have become aware of the ability to communicate on a mental plane then it becomes a matter of application and practice.

The voice has it place, of course. It is a real 'help' in calming the fractious and the impetuous or, conversely, in encouraging the hesitant and fearful and reprimanding the recalcitrant. However, it is an insufficiently sophisticated and subtle instrument with which to obtain more than a limited response.

The physical aids, however, provide a system of communication which can reach a very high level of sensitivity, their application, if sufficiently skilful, embracing the most delicate gradations of expression.

The effectiveness of this physical language of riding depends as much on the horse as the rider. Before the horse can respond to the aids he has first to be taught their meaning and the reactions which are expected of him and, of course, he has to be physically capable of compliance. In brief, unless both partners are reasonably fluent in the same language and are additionally physically able to express their requirement on the one hand

and to respond upon the other, there are bound to be difficulties in the lines of communication.

Paramount in the aid combination is the leg, the principal forward driving aid. The legs control the quarters and hindlegs, the power-house of the horse. By acting to drive the hindlegs under the body they create the necessary propulsive thrust which results in *impulsion*. The legs also control the position of the quarters holding them in place and preventing their deviation to one side or the other. Indeed, until we have control of the quarters we cannot have control of the horse. Additionally, each leg governs the movement of the corresponding hindleg. On the circle, for instance, the rider's inside leg works to encourage full engagement of the horse's inside hindleg and is supported by its outside partner. (The optimum moment for applying the aid is just as the leg is brought forward to touch the ground, when it will encourage a more vigorous engagement. However, in order to apply the aid to its maximum effect it is necessary for the rider to appreciate the position of the leg at a given moment. With application and some practice this 'feel' for the movement can be developed. In fact, the movement is felt though the seat bones, once the rider has learned how to *listen*. A profitable exercise to improve one's ability to 'feel' the movement is to have someone in the school area to walk with the horse and to call as the hindleg is about to touch down.)

It is very probable that many riders are unable to communicate through their legs in anything more than the most rudimentary fashion. However, once the physical ability has been developed it is possible for the leg to be used with great precision and to communicate with the utmost clarity. Of course, it has to be used carefully, otherwise its potential to confuse is immeasurable. Legs that swing about irrelevantly transmit an unintelligible message to the horse. They must be *still* if they are not to cause confusion, and even that instruction can be somewhat misleading. The effective leg contrives to be *still* and to *move* at the same time – and that paradox applies equally to the hand. The leg moves in the sense that it responds to the movement of the horse's flank, and that requires it to be very supple throughout its length.

To obtain the best results the legs are applied in a number of prescribed pressures at certain points on the horse's body. One gifted teacher likens those points to a series of *buttons set on a control panel* fitted around the lower part of the girth.

The most important of these is the *impulsion* button which we can call Button A. It is situated at the rear edge of the girth and is activated by the leg exerting a smooth, inward squeeze that

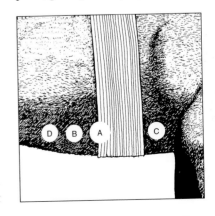

The control panel. A is the impulsion, *driving button. B is the button controlling the quarters – it is used in lateral work, rein-back and in support of the driving leg on the circle etc. C is the expert's button for the encouragement of extension and D is used in the advanced movements of* piaffe, passage *and* flying changes.

rolls slightly forward against the lie of the coat. This inward, forward rolling motion of the leg is effective because it does not disturb the seat and it acts on the most sensitive part of the horse. It has the further advantage of being logical – why on Earth push backwards when you want to go forwards?

Smoothness in the application of the leg is a paramount quality since an abrupt action produces a corresponding response, whereas a smooth aid results in a smooth movement. The most frequent mistake is for the rider to turn out the toe so that the back of the calf is employed on the horse. Naturally, this action disturbs the seat and will certainly disturb the horse more than somewhat if a spur is worn.

Quite distinct from the inward, forward push of both legs is the action of the single leg, which is applied on Button B, the point behind the girth and to the rear of Button A. The leg is put on in a direct inward squeeze and is used in conjunction with its partner to:

(1) move the quarters
(2) resist unwanted shifts in those parts
(3) in lateral work
(4) assist in holding the quarters as the outside leg in changes of direction and at canter.

The spur is a legitimate part of the communicative system when the rider has learnt how to keep the leg still.

Both legs are put on at B when asking for the rein-back.

During the secondary training of the horse, the level of performance relevant to the majority of riders, these are the two all-important buttons and the legs must make a clear distinction between the two if the horse is not to become confused.

Button D is necessary for the advanced movements – the flying changes, *piaffe*, and *passage* – and Button C, in front of the girth, may be employed by the very expert who can use a gently digging toe behind the elbow to encourage greater extension.

The hands represent the principal aid of restraint. Long ago, great emphasis was placed on 'good hands', but today's teaching, despite all the advance in the understanding (or, perhaps, the discovery) of riding as a rational science, is less concerned with 'good hands' and sometimes too much obsessed with a misunderstanding of *contact*. Good hands, it was held, give as the horse takes and vice versa – hence the old 'give-and-take' philosophy of the earlier Anglo-Saxon riding manuals. The concept of the *educated* hand on the educated horse is just the opposite: it *takes as the horse takes and rewards by yielding as the horse gives*. Used with some subtlety, in conjunction with legs and seat, it produces a soft, round outline in which the 'powers of the horse' are 'managed and directed' to the best effect. The

(Opposite):
The inside leg drives the horse forward into the outside hand whilst weighting the inside stirrup iron and seat bone in preparation for the turn to the right. The outside leg is held in its supportive role.

hands, the educated, good hands, receive the impulsion created by the legs. They regulate the created energy, containing or releasing it to the required degree. In the former instance, there is a shortening of the base, in the latter an increase in the extension of the stride.

It is also possible for the educated hand to *re-channel* the energy created by the legs, as when a rein, or hand, is applied to block the surge of forward movement and re-direct it to one side or the other.

In the most basic of terms, the hands combine, with the legs, to fulfil the functions of brake and steering wheel. Expanding that simplification we can regard the hands as maintaining the *balanced* forward movement of the horse – in the last analysis they are the regulators of the balance.

The Nirvana of the equestrian art and of the 'classical' Masters is when the reins, regulating the balance, control the direction of the movement, including the lateral work, whilst the legs supply the impulsion.

The aim of the thinking rider is to find the balance between the driving aids of the legs and seat and the restraining aid of the hands that results in movement contained within the most effective outline. In other words the horse moves within the frame imposed by the legs at one end and the hands at the other. The most frequent mistake made by ambitious riders anxious to obtain an outline that will satisfy the dressage judge (but may very well not) is to force a false outline, bringing the head inwards with over-dominant hands and neglecting to obtain the roundness that comes from actively engaging the hindlegs. In this instance the rider forces *the head to retreat towards the quarters instead of encouraging the quarters to advance to the head*.

THOUGHT BEFORE ACTION, LEGS BEFORE HANDS.

Hands operate in the preparatory role by the momentary closure of the fingers squeezing the reins combining with the brief inward pressure of the legs. They act by the fingers opening to allow movement forward or by closing to restrain, or *contain*, it.

Hands can control direction and govern the movement of both shoulder and quarters by operating in one or more of the five rein effects, which sounds both very advanced and very complicated but is neither of the two. What is more the five rein effects have been appreciated, understood and practised, even if the basically French nomenclature was unfamiliar, ever since riding moved out of the area of an instinctive accomplishment.

There are many more possible rein aids but these five are

generally recognised in academic equitation.

(1) The Direct or Opening Rein
(2) The Indirect Rein
(3) The Direct Rein of Opposition
(4) The Indirect Rein of Opposition *in front* of the withers
(5) The Indirect Rein of Opposition *behind* the withers.

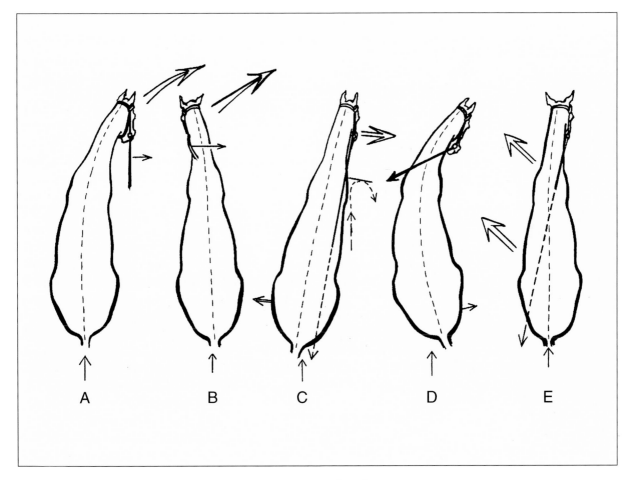

The last rein is often termed *intermediary* or *intermediate* because it comes between the third and fourth effects by acting on *both* shoulder and quarters.

The third rein effect shifts only the quarters, whilst the fourth moves the shoulder.

Direct reins act on the same side of the horse as they are applied. *Indirect* reins influence the opposite side of the horse.

Reins of opposition block and re-direct the forward movement through the shoulder or the quarters or, in the fifth rein effect, through both.

The *direct or opening rein* is applied by the hand being carried

The rein effects.
The five rein effects used in positioning the horse.
From left: A. Direct or Opening Rein; B. Indirect Rein; C. Direct Rein of Opposition; D. Indirect Rein of Opposition in Front of the Withers; E. Indirect Rein of Opposition Behind the Withers (also known as the intermediary or intermediate rein).

outward in the direction of the movement. It is used on turns and circles where the horse is bent to the inside and aligned to the direction of the movement.

The *indirect rein* is a neck rein moving the opposite shoulder forward, i.e. the application of the left indirect rein moves the right shoulder forward and to the right. It is used on turns and circles requiring the bend to be to the outside, as in the turn on the forehand. It may also be used in an effective corrective capacity.

The *direct rein of opposition* blocks the forward movement on the side to which it is applied. If, for instance, the right rein is used in this effect, the thrust is blocked on the right side of the mouth. As a result the quarters are compelled to shift to the left. Logically, the rein is used in the forehand turn and, with both reins, in the rein-back, where sustained movement forward is necessarily reversed.

Illogically, this rein of opposition is used frequently in making turns and riding circles. It then restricts the movement of the shoulder and causes the quarters to be moved outwards, off the track made by the forefeet. In that situation the instruction used to be, and I suspect it may still be given in some parts, to counter the shift of the quarters by applying the outside leg – a contradiction of applied forces if ever there was, since the aids are being used in opposition to each other! It is nonetheless, a most common mistake and one that is as much responsible for impeding the stride and the movement as any.

The fourth effect, *the rein of opposition in front of the withers*, moves the shoulders left or right according to which rein is applied. This, however, is accompanied by a secondary movement which shifts the quarters in the opposite direction. The result of applying the rein in this fashion is to turn the horse on the centre (i.e. on the axis of a line through the stirrup leather) the bend being to the outside. It is also a means of correcting the position of the shoulder should it deviate from the required track.

The final *rein of opposition behind the withers*, the hand being directed to the horse's opposite hip, *without it crossing the withers*, is the intermediary rein, eulogised in the equestrian Valhalla as the Queen of Reins. It moves the whole horse sideways and forwards by acting on both shoulder and quarters. It is used in leg-yielding and in the shoulder-in movement.

The success of these rein effects depends entirely on ample and sustained impulsion, without it the horse becomes like a boat becalmed.

What has to be remembered is that the reins, in perfection, blend together, no one rein can be used in isolation. It has to be supported and complemented by its partner whilst always being subordinate to the leg.

Perhaps the greatest benefit the rider obtains by understanding this rein combination is to be able to recognise when the reins are being used incorrectly or even in contradiction to the movement required.

Possibly, the most blatant error the hand can commit, other than the most heinous crime of being taken backwards, is to take the rein across the withers, an action which prevents the execution of any sort of free movement but is, nonetheless, all too evident. (Hands may move up, down and sideways according to the circumstance, but if the hand pulls the rein to the rear the pace is immediately interrupted, the balance affected and the stride shortened on the side on which the rein is applied.)

Seat, back and weight distribution represent a potent force within the aid combination.

So long as the rider sits with an open, spread seat with the trunk erect and without tensing the muscles of the buttocks (tensing these muscles raises the seat preventing the rider from sitting deep), and so long as the hips lead the movement, it is possible to apply a powerful, driving aid – but there are dangers. No self-respecting Thoroughbred horse, for instance, would accept the exaggerated back-seat-driving position employed by some otherwise skilful dressage riders of the European mainland, nor would he appreciate seat bones driving *downwards* into his back instead of pushing *upwards* and *forwards*. The result on a well-bred, sensitive animal would be for him to react with a hollowed back, losing the propulsive thrust of the quarters and possibly coming above the bit – and, indeed, if he were to deposit his tormentor with an explosive buck, who could do otherwise than applaud the action?

Correctly executed, however, the bracing (or perhaps more aptly, the *stretching*) of the back combined with the aids of leg and hand can produce a significant effect on both collection and extension by increasing the energetic engagement of the quarters.

In fact, in collection, the very slight inclination of the shoulders to the rear alters the weight distribution and actually encourages the horse to move his weight further over the quarters so as to conform with the minimally altered weight distribution.

In lateral movements and changes of direction the horse is actually assisted by the rider weighting the inside seat bone so as to remain in balance with the lateral shift of the horse's centre of gravity. Indeed, the experienced rider, will deliberately use the weight aid to put the horse in a position where it is he who must alter his centre of gravity to conform with the altered weight distribution.

(Next Page):
Placing the weight to the right by pressing down on the right stirrup iron. However, the trunk remains square and upright with no suspicion of the body collapsing at the waist.

Chapter 3
The Saddle

The first requirement of the saddle is that it should be a positive encouragement to the rider's adoption of an effective balanced seat. The second, which is of equal importance, is that it should fit the horse in so exemplary a fashion that it causes no restriction whatsoever to the animal's freedom of movement.

Frankly, if the design of the saddle makes it difficult for the rider to adopt and maintain a proper seat it is inevitable that the horse will be restricted. The problem will then be made manifest to some degree or another in a hollowed outline, a lack of engagement in the hindlegs and a shortening of the stride – in brief, a significant reduction occurs in the quality of the action.

Conversely, if the saddle is uncomfortable for the horse, he will seek to evade the discomfort by resistance, even if the rider sits like a centaur – which is unlikely.

In one of his 'sportin' lectors', Mr Jorrocks was moved to observe, 'Eavens, wot a lot of rubbish has been written about 'osses'. (John Jorrocks MFH the Cockney grocer of Gt Coram Street, was the creation of R.S. Surtees (1803–64) and the hero of his series of satirical hunting novels. This quotation is taken from *Handley Cross, or Mr Jorrocks's Hunt*.) He could have said the same thing about saddles, even though the principles involved in their construction and fitting are well-proven and have been established certainly since the mid-nineteenth century. Whether they have been as well practised is less certain.

Fortunately, there is now a greater awareness of the saddle as being a critical factor in the business of riding, but there are, nonetheless, a number of very unsatisfactory products about, and not all of them are of Asian origin.

On the other hand, just as there are 'false prophets' in the field of riding instruction, so there are opportunists on the saddlery band wagon who cause confusion and misunderstanding. In fairness, most of them are well meaning and some of them have a positive contribution to make, even if they are sometimes guilty of some pretty gross overstatements. The danger of overstating 'saddle-awareness' is to create a hypercritical attitude in the less accomplished that can become counter-productive.

There are riders who are all too quick to blame the saddle for their own deficiencies.

If the horse's performance or way of going does not measure up to their expectations they blame it on the saddle. Stiffness in the horse's back and almost every sort of equine resistance is attributed to the same root cause. It is usually a case of the bad workman blaming his tools, but that is not much consolation to the saddler, who is, by and large, competent and experienced.

The best advice that can be given is to go to a reputable saddler, who is a member of a recognised trade association, and have him fit the saddle to the horse. If the instructor can be there to observe the effect of the new saddle on the horse's action, so much the better. Of course, it goes without saying that the instructor must be sufficiently knowledgeable about both the design of the saddle and the structure of the horse's back to make a constructive assessment. Most of them are probably competent enough in this area, but some are not, and that is another reason for going to a qualified teacher.

Fitting the horse

Obviously, fitting the saddle is governed by the conformation of the back, which extends from the last bone of the neck to the last of the ribs. For the purpose of saddle fitting the back is considered to be that part from the rearmost position taken up by the scapula (shoulderblade) in movement to the last rib.

The relationship between the saddle and the scapula is criti-

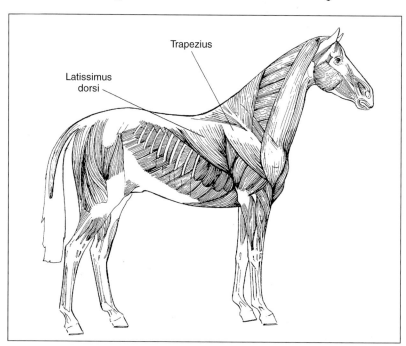

Well-developed musculature in the correctly proportioned horse allows the saddle to sit behind the big trapezius muscle.

Trapezius

Latissimus dorsi

cal and is all too often insufficiently appreciated by riders. If the saddle is cut in such a way as to impinge upon the movement of the scapula it will restrict the action and, in consequence, the performance potential. Indeed, in some instances, particularly when the slope of the scapula is less than desirable, the horse will not only shorten the stride, but may also begin to stumble more or less seriously.

This is just one factor governing the position and shape of the saddle. Otherwise it will rest on either side of the backbone, on the ribs and on the big muscle covering them. If that muscle is well developed and well nourished then the skin and the bone are protected from injury. Without adequate muscle development, the saddle and the weight of the rider would bear directly on the bone, with disastrous results: the blood supply to the skin would be cut off as a result of the pressure, the skin would die and it is possible for galling to occur.

The War Office manual, *Animal Management 1933*, which remains in its essentials entirely relevant and stands even now as the supreme treatise of horse-mastership, contains this pertinent sentence: 'the construction of the back is such that it lends itself to injury, and invites trouble by the very peculiarity and delicacy of its organisation'. (In the previous paragraph the manual had ruefully observed that had horses been intended to carry weight or pull a load some special protection would have been supplied for the purpose – an acknowledgement, one might think, of some superior force that knows better than us?)

Of course, the difficulty is compounded by the widely varying conformation of the equine back structure. If the conformation of the back is within reasonable parameters, correct in terms of proportion, symmetry and the strength of the components, there should be no real problem for the specialist in saddle fitting. When the opposite pertains the matter becomes correspondingly complex and it is very much more difficult to arrive at an acceptable solution.

However good the saddle and however competent the fitter, neither can compensate for pronounced conformational deficiencies.

There are six commandments relative to the fitting of the saddle:
(1) *With the rider in position there has to be absolute clearance of the spine along its length and across its width.*

The fore-arch must clear the withers to the extent that it is possible to insert three fingers between the two. Similarly there must be no direct pressure at the cantle and the seat should not be so dipped that it comes into contact with the backbone at its deepest part under the rider's seat bones.

A useful sort of middle-of-the-road saddle that positions the rider centrally and is not unduly exaggerated in any way.

An excellent example of a dressage saddle that fulfils all the required criteria.

The panel of a jumping saddle with supports for the upper thigh and a rear squab to assist the leg position.

Rear view of a jumping saddle showing a channel of such width that it allows complete freedom to the spinal process.

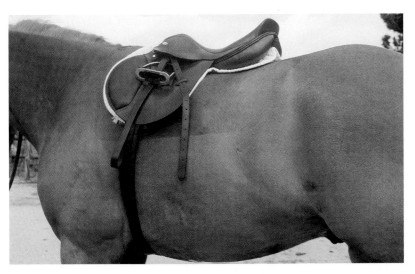

Another jumping model that give a high degree of security and positions the rider in balance.

The panel design eliminates bulk under the thigh, allowing the closest possible contact.

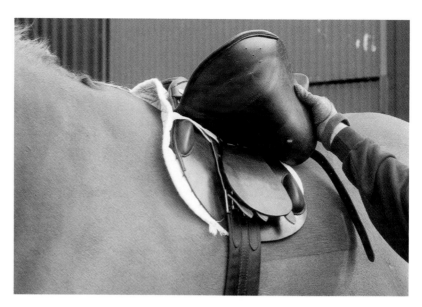

The dressage saddle in position. It is easy to see how well the seat positions the rider.

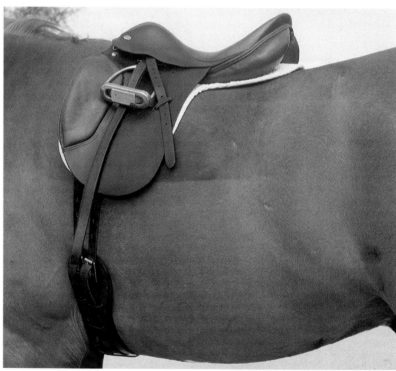

Clearance across the width of the vertebrae is obtained by the channel dividing the two sides of the panel being sufficiently wide to allow not only for the upper spinous process but for the much wider base as well, even though that may seem to be well-protected by flesh.

For the channel to be broad enough it needs to be at least 6.25–7.5cm (2.5–3.0in) wide *throughout* its length.

(2) The saddle at the forward edge of the panel must not interfere with the movement of the scapula.

On the well-made horse the problem should not arise so long as the cut of the panel is not exaggerated. However, Arab horses and some Arab crosses may need particular attention in this respect. It is not that the Arab shoulder is upright, but it is *different* in respect of its juncture with the humerus and in relation to the withers, which are not always so clearly defined as in the Thoroughbred type of horse, for instance.

(3) The panel has to bear evenly upon the back in its entirety and to cover as large an area as possible, so as to distribute the rider's weight over the whole bearing surface.

Weight is concentrated over too small an area:

a) If the saddle is excessively dipped, when the greater part of the weight is carried over the waist.
b) If the panel is narrowed so much at the waist as to reduce the extent of the overall bearing surface. (The purpose of the wasp-waisted panel was to afford a *narrow* grip that would not spread the rider's thighs. It sounds to be a reasonable supposition, but if combined with a notably dipped seat there is no doubt that it caused the weight to be concentrated over a very small portion of the panel's available bearing surface.)
c) If the seat is too short or is insufficiently wide for the rider, that is, if the plate is too small for the joint.

Where pressure is exerted over a small area it will prevent the circulation of blood and if it does not cause visible galling it will result in deep-seated bruising, which is as bad and in the long term probably worse.

(4) The panel must be in longitudinal and lateral balance and the tree, the foundation of the saddle, must be 'true' and not twisted.

The saddle will be out of longitudinal balance if it is stuffed more at one end than the other, and a panel stuffed more heavily on one side will create a lateral imbalance. Both will affect the rider's position and inhibit the movement, and both may cause bruising.

A twist is more likely to occur in laminated spring trees, i.e. those trees fitted with two sections of spring steel laid along the frame from head to cantle to give greater resilience to the seat. Obviously a twist throws the saddle and the rider out of balance. A twist may be the fault of either the tree- or saddle-maker but is just as likely to be caused by a rider grasping the cantle with the right hand when mounting.

Riders also contribute to lateral imbalance by sitting more heavily on one seat bone than the other, often collapsing a hip to compound the fault, or they may just be riding with leathers of unequal length – and it happens more frequently than might be supposed.

(5) *The panel must be free from irregularities.*
The smallest lump on the surface of the panel causes a pressure point capable of producing a sore back – a wrinkle in a sock will cause the human similar discomfort.

(6) *The saddle should fit as close to the back as possible whilst meeting the other fitting criteria.*
Saddles stuffed too high off the back cause friction because they tend to move from side to side. Friction, like pressure, is a source of discomfort and possible injury.

Effect of conditioning and training

Horses in poor condition are more likely to suffer injury from a badly fitting saddle than those strongly muscled over the back. Fat horses, of course, are soft in condition and gall easily for that reason.

The level of training is particularly relevant to successful saddle fitting. In the schooled horse there is equal muscular development on both sides of the spine, or nearly so, and this is an obvious advantage in maintaining the saddle's lateral balance.

An incorrectly schooled horse, or just an unschooled one, will almost always show pronounced development on one side of the back, usually on the offside of the body. The animal then turns easily to the left but has difficulty in bending the other way because that movement is obstructed by a block of near inflexible muscle.

Schooled horses do not overburden the forehand, more of the weight being carried over engaged quarters. As a result there is very much less likelihood of the saddle slipping forward. Movement in the accepted rounded outline contributes to the saddle remaining firmly in place. Hollow-backed animals, carrying the head above the bit, and probably ewe-necked into the bargain, invite even the very best saddles to move forward often causing the girth to chafe behind the elbow.

Considering the rider

The horse's comfort has to be paramount but it is just as important to ensure the comfort and security of the rider. Fortunately, this is a time of saddle awareness and manufacturers are very conscious of the need to produce the *immediate-comfort* saddle.

(Gone are the days when the country's leading saddlers had arrangements with selected riding schools to take new saddles to be 'ridden-in' for their customers, whilst the curt dismissal of the rider's needs contained in *Animal Management 1933* would be wholly unacceptable in our modern climate – the offending sentence in the manual reads, 'The seat is a convenience for the rider; a blanket laid over the tree would do as well.')

Indeed, manufacturers have gone even further, some of the more enlightened recognising that the instant comfort saddle must also be *female-friendly*.

One does not need to be qualified in the study of human anatomy to appreciate the pronounced difference in the construction of the male and female pelvis. In the latter the pubic arch is broad and rounded, whilst the male conformation is narrower with the inferior pubic arch almost triangular in shape.

Until quite recently many authorities held that a narrow twist (waist) to the saddle, produced by narrowing both the tree and the subsequent panel in that area, helped the rider to sit deep and prevented the spread of the upper thigh. Modern saddle construction calls for a much broader waist to the tree, the bars of which are turned, almost flattened, to follow the contour of the horse's back and, in consequence, the panel must also be broader. So long as the head (pommel) of the saddle is relatively flat this construction is without much doubt very comfortable for the lady rider and, in fact, does not appear to bother the male either. Where it can go wrong is when the head of the saddle is built up too high, a failing which occurs mostly with cut-back trees. Men seem able to cope with a relatively high pommel better than females, who are encouraged to push the seat back-wards to avoid the uncomfortable pressure against the pubic arch.

Nonetheless, there are well-constructed and -designed saddles, some of them in the highest price range, that do not find universal favour. The point has been made that the poorly conditioned horse creates fitting problems. Similarly, novice riders can have problems with specialist, precision saddles as a result of their own inexperience. In short, the saddle is too advanced for their standard of riding. Some of the dressage saddles come into this category as well as the flattish seated 'close-contact' saddles made for both showjumping and eventing.

For those of limited experience (and how many will admit to being so) the good quality, middle-of-the-road saddle is the best choice.

Chapter 4

The Bridle

For the purpose of the work described, a simple snaffle bridle with the addition of one or other of the nosebands shown will be sufficient.

The variety of snaffle bits available is enormous but whatever the construction the action remains fundamentally the same throughout this diverse bitting group. Differences in the mouthpiece can be seen as efforts to make the bit *speak louder or more clearly* or, perhaps, with an altered accent. On the whole, the simpler the bit's construction the greater is the likelihood of its being effective.

Action

The primary action of the snaffle is upwards against the corners of the lips and in that sense it is considered to encourage the young, unmade horse to raise the head.

However, it is a little more complex than that, since the action will depend very largely on the auxiliary, principally the type of noseband, with which it is used. (The other auxiliary affecting the action of the bit is the martingale. We have not found it necessary as a schooling aid but, of course, it has its place in the control syndrome and it is certainly useful on some horses.)

Whilst the action of the bit is altered by the use of a noseband, which, additionally, prevents some pertinent evasions, it also changes in accordance with the outline assumed during the course of training.

Whilst the young horse is long, low and probably more on its forehand than otherwise, the snaffle certainly works against the corners of the lips in a lifting action. As we get nearer to a working outline, obtaining greater engagement of the hindlegs, the head, neck (and shoulder) are raised and the nose is retracted nearer to the vertical plane. In that position the snaffle acts more across the lower jaw, exerting less upward pressure on the corners of the lips.

In the more advanced horse carrying the head on, or very close to, the vertical, the action across the lower jaw is much increased, although a slight upward movement against the lips is still possible.

When the bit acts 'across the lower jaw' the mouthpiece bears on the tongue and over the bars of the mouth (the area of gum between the molar and incisor teeth). To what extent it bears on either depends on the type of bit used and the size and shape of the tongue. With a conventional snaffle mouthpiece the tongue, almost without exception, overlaps the bars by a little and thus protects the potentially sensitive gum from direct pressure by the bit.

In simplistic terms the snaffle group is divided between straight bar or mullen (half-moon) mouthpieces and the more usual jointed mouth made with either a single joint or with a central spatula, or a ring link, separating the two halves of the mouthpiece.

A sub-division is between the loose-ring snaffle and that fitted with an *egg-butt* or *Dee-cheek*. The last two certainly obviate the danger of pinching and a further advantage is that the horse cannot evade the action by sliding the bit through his mouth. On the other hand, the construction limits the possible move-ment and might discourage the horse from keeping the mouth wet by 'playing' with the mouthpiece and making saliva. This, of course, would be an undesirable feature if the horse was inclined to be dry in his mouth for that condition induces stiff-ness in the lower jaw rather than relaxation.

The modern egg-butt ring derives from the Dee-cheek racing snaffle which, in turn, was a modification of the *full cheek snaffle*. The latter is now represented by the Australian loose-ring cheek snaffle, still known occasionally as the Fulmer snaffle.

Like the egg-butt, the cheek snaffle cannot slide through the mouth but unlike that pattern its loose ring does allow the horse to 'mouth' his bit. Additionally, the cheeks pressing against the face, encourage lateral movement of the head.

The horses depicted in the book were schooled largely in 'French bradoons' which have a central spatula connecting the two parts of the mouthpiece. It is a comfortable bit which by reason of the spatula lying on the tongue reduces the stronger, nutcracker action of the conventional jointed snaffle.

As a 'change' bit, should the horse become over-enthusiastic when jumping or going cross-country, a light Dee-cheek jointed snaffle is sometimes used. The type favoured is that with small rollers, often of copper, set round the mouthpiece.

Copper, iron and plastic mouthpieces (the latter occasionally impregnated with the taste of apples) are fashionable materials for the present and are held to be softer and more comfortable in the mouth.

The noseband

The addition of a noseband alters the complexion of the bit materially by ensuring that the bit acts centrally in the mouth and by exerting a restraining pressure on the nose which assists the positioning of the head.

Even the plain cavesson noseband will support the action of the bit to a considerable extent if properly adjusted. The *caveçon* in the nineteenth-century cavalry arms was used, as its name implies, as a halter and played no part in the bitting arrangement. In consequence, the manuals, even very recent ones, lay down that it should be fitted so that the nosepiece allows for the insertion of two fingers which for the sake of uniformity in a troop of cavalry is fine. Adjusted in this fashion it will also provide a convenient anchorage for a standing martingale, if that item of saddlery is employed. In that role it does, of course, assist and influence the action of the bit by preventing the horse from throwing his head in the air.

The standing martingale is very much out of fashion in modern equestrian thinking but there is still a use for the plain cavesson. Apart from the matter of appearance, it is possible to use it to close the mouth, or to do so partially, by dropping the head strap a hole and fitting the nosepiece very snugly. By closing the mouth the central action of the bit over the lower jaw is preserved and it is made more difficult for the horse to evade the pressures it applies. However, the mouth will be more effectively closed by a noseband fastening beneath the bit and such an arrangement will also apply restraint to the nose.

One can use either a drop noseband of the conventional pattern or as an alternative, producing a less direct action, the Flash or Grakle noseband.

The drop noseband is fitted with the nosepiece 6.5–7.5cm (2.6–3.0in) above the nostrils on the end of the nasal bone, an adjustment which is only possible if the rear strap, fastening under the bit, is sufficiently long. If the noseband is fitted any lower it causes discomfort and obstructs the intake of air into the nasal passages.

The drop closes the mouth almost completely and properly used produces a flexion at the poll and, so far as the encircling strap allows, in the lower jaw, also.

It follows that pressure from the rein is transmitted to the nose, since the mouth is shut. In consequence the nose is retracted and the face will be held *nearer* to the vertical with flexion at the poll.

Used firmly on a strong-pulling horse, the nose pressure does, without doubt, cause a momentary disruption of the breathing. As a result the nose is dropped, the bit acts decisively over the lower jaw and the rider's control is increased.

Less overtly coercive is the Flash, which closes the mouth, if not so effectively, but avoids much of the nose pressure of the drop noseband.

The Grakle, on the other hand, retains some pressure on the nose but the point of pressure is considerably higher; furthermore whilst closing the mouth it also acts in countering one of the more pernicious equine bit evasions, that of crossing the jaw.

Fitting the bridle

Just as there are rules for the fitting of the saddle so there are for the proper adjustment of the bridle. The two critical points are the browband and throatlatch.

If the browband is too short it will pull the bridle head against the back of ears causing discomfort and a resentment that may lead to habitual headshaking. Allow for the insertion of one finger between browband and forehead and for the browband to be fitted 25mm (1in) lower than the base of the ears.

A throatlatch adjusted too tightly throttles the poor horse. It restricts the breathing, discourages flexion at the poll and can lead to other seemingly unrelated resistances born out of a very natural resentment. Allow for the insertion of three fingers between the throatlatch and the gullet.

The bit should fit snugly to the cheeks, the butt-ends of a loose-ring snaffle, for instance, projecting no more that 13mm (0.5in) on either side of the mouth.

Most snaffles are too wide, which facilitates their being slid across the mouth when the mouthpiece can cause bruising to the tongue, bars and lips on the affected side. Additionally, too wide a jointed snaffle may bear painfully on the roof of the mouth, a contact intensified when it is used in conjunction with a drop noseband preventing the mouth from being opened.

Too wide a bit will also be liable to come up against the incisor teeth, and that will almost certainly happen if the bit is adjusted too low in the mouth. The bit is correctly fitted when the corners of the lips are wrinkled in a smile or even a grin.

Finally, discard the light, thin rein. It is much better to use something heavier. A thin, bootlace sort of rein may look elegant but it encourages riders to grip hard with the fingers. The heavier rein allows a much lighter contact.

As a postscript take heed again of Francis Dwyer, the Major of Austrian Imperial Cavalry:

'nothing can be more certain than the best bitting in the world is wholly useless, nay, sometimes dangerous, in bad, that is to say, heavy or rude hands.'

Chapter 5

Fit To Ride

Since communication is so closely linked with physical contact and mental discipline it follows that it will be more or less effective according to the development of those qualities and the rider's ability to use both sympathetically and reciprocally.

Physical fitness

Riding is an athletic exercise in which great emphasis is placed on the physical and gymnastic conditioning of the horse. If that is to be used to the full extent then obviously the rider must have attained a standard of fitness which is at least commensurate with that of the horse, and that applies just as much to the 'weekend' rider, which so many of us are, as to anyone else. Anything less, indeed, is a negation of all the effort required to bring a horse into condition for specific purposes.

Indeed, for anything beyond gentle hacking, the process involved in conditioning the horse and schooling him for the levels required in competition demands physical fitness in the rider of a high order. From the fit body comes the alert, receptive, disciplined mind.

For the young the possession of the sound (fit) body should present little difficulty, but it is sometimes harder for them to acquire the fluency of the calm and disciplined mind. As 'Time's winged chariot' comes closer the opposite may apply.

Physical fitness combines regular exercise – in this instance relative to the chosen pursuit – and a *sensible diet*.

To be physically fit, whatever the level of our riding, we must be *supple*, *strong* and have *stamina*, then we can begin to ride with decreasing tension and we will not suffer from aches and pains after taking the exercise.

Tension is the arch enemy in every sort of athletic pursuit, but it is particularly damaging to the rider because his 'equipment', unlike that of the golfer or tennis player, is an animate being, the horse, who, in the wink of an eyelid, reflects the rider's tension in the stiffening of his own body and movement.

To be able to apply the physical aids harmoniously the rider needs to be *supple* from neck to shoulder, through the arm and right down to the fingers. Supple, too, in the ankle and the knee to permit the independent use of the lower leg, and, very importantly, supple in the waist so as to allow movement in the pelvis and legs without disturbing the posture of the upper body.

Strength is equally important. The *strong* rider has an obvious advantage over the one who is physically weak and, therefore, becomes insecure so much more easily. Losses of security and balance result in a commensurate loss of co-ordination and in every instance cause an over-reaction, which is usually made through the reins. Gentleness, feel and sympathy in our physical communication with the horse can only be developed through strength.

Stamina, too, has to be developed in order that physical effort can be maintained consistently.

At the centre of any programme of fitness are an efficient heart and lungs and some really strong abdominal muscles.

The first two are virtually inter-dependent and to extend their efficiency the concern is simply with an improved oxygen intake. By exercising we use up oxygen and the more we use regularly the better we exercise, and the more efficient become our lungs and our heart (which is just as much a muscle as the calf and in the same way needs exercise if it is to be kept in good order).

The development of the abdominal muscles has a lot to do with our *posture*. Sagging tummies, the mark of twentieth-century man and woman, particularly those belonging to the Western world, are at the root of postural faults. They are accompanied, in the saddle, by that objectionable protruding bottom, slouching shoulders and terrible stiffness in the spine and waist. Harmony between horse and rider is then impossible. To develop and maintain firm stomach muscles is thus of enormous importance and plays a considerable part in riders' exercise programmes.

This chapter includes exercises in the suppleness, strength and stamina categories and suggests how many times each one should be done each day.

However, do start gradually and do consult a doctor if you have any history of heart trouble etc., or if you are over forty or overweight. If you are over forty (or even fifty) remember that the stiffness of advancing years is a nasty rumour being spread about by a lot of older people who cannot move.

Mounted exercises on the lunge

Physical fitness achieved by sensible eating and regular exercise provides a sure base for future work in the progression towards the complete rider. It is, however, no more than the first stage.

The second stage is to relate the physically fit rider to the movement of the horse. By being physically fit, balance, co-ordination and the ability to sit in a relaxed and effective posture is only made easier. Fitness does not automatically confer the attributes necessary for riding horses but it provides the means by which they can be acquired. The next stage in the development of the rider is the exercises to be practised on the lunge.

These mounted lessons represent the foundation of the rider's training, they are the equitational equivalent of the three Rs. For their full potential to be realised, however, a horse that is well schooled on the lunge is an essential requirement and he must have, in addition, smooth, easy paces. Probably, this is one of the reasons why mounted lunge lessons are so neglected in the general system of training practised in Britain, for instance, and, one suspects, in the English-speaking world generally, although their inherent value in establishing the rider's seat and posture is well recognised in the countries of the European mainland.

Lunge exercises are hard work for the horse and if not performed correctly they can be inhibiting to the movement. Furthermore, the horse has to be temperamentally suited to going round in endless circles. Indeed, the lunge horse requires careful, intelligent management if he is not to become fed up with the whole operation. As a result, one imagines, few schools train and keep these invaluable schoolmaster horses. (If they did, their pupils might ride better than they do.)

The second requirement is an experienced and skilled instructor, able to derive the most benefit for the pupil from the lessons.

The lunge exercises should be carried out in parallel with regular ground exercises, the latter being performed as part of daily routine.

In a perfect world where time is of no consequence the lunge lessons should also be on a daily basis and over a period of 12 months their duration should be extended to some 40–45 minutes – but that presupposes in addition that we have a horse capable of working on the circle for that length of time.

For most of us, two lessons each week is a more possible objective. For the first lessons 15 minutes is sufficient, the duration being increased over a week or so to a full half-hour.

Lunge lessons are discussed later in this chapter.

The mental influence

Underlying the exercises designed to increase the rider's physical capacity is the development of the rider's ability to project a mental influence, an ability which is dependent, when mounted, upon the efficiency of the physical system. Until that is at a high level, mental communication is going to be haphazard, momentary imbalance in the body and occasional stiffness causing similar interruptions in the mind. The increase in the rider's powers of concentration and the development of a quietly positive attitude is acquired gradually and depends a lot on the personality of the individual.

As a guide to that most desirable accomplishment it may be helpful to reflect on the qualities necessary in the make-up of the ultimate horseman or horsewoman.

My list includes these five attributes:

* Intelligence
* Sensitivity
* Self-discipline
* Patience
* Positive attitude.

The first varies in quality between one person and another and, indeed, normally intelligent people in one field can be very unintelligent in another. A lot of otherwise intelligent people, for example, can be extraordinarily stupid when it come to dealing with horses. It arises, I believe, from thoughtlessness, unfamiliarity and ignorance about the animal with which they are dealing. In consequence there are a lot of mistaken ideas and attitudes.

As people acquire more knowledge they begin to treat horses more intelligently. To be *sensitive*, in the way that one can be appreciative of the moods and feelings of people as well as animals relies, perhaps, as much on being considerate to others as on anything else. It is without doubt a quality which can be cultivated and horsemen need very much to increase their sensitivity to their equine partners.

Self-discipline is a more obvious requirement. Without it we cannot expect to exert discipline, or command the respect of either men or horses. Those unable to control their tempers or their irritation have no place with horses – at least, not until they have applied themselves to the problem and learnt self-discipline. It is by no mean impossible.

Patience may indeed stem, in part, from our ability to discipline our minds and feelings. It is in any case, a prime requirement.

Then there is that *positive attitude* – the core of steel which makes actions decisive. The negative approach (I call it pussyfooting) is always non-productive with horses, who become unsure of themselves and of their handlers, too, when they discern a less than positive state of mind. There is, however, no need to take a course of Pelmanism in order to think positively – with conscious practice it becomes habitual. But there is another side. It is possible that in developing our positive, dynamic personality we do so at the expense of sensitivity and become so dominant that we can no longer be receptive.

Once, of course, we acquire the skills which enable us to communicate through our minds as well as our bodies we approach the ultimate requirement of the complete horseman – the ability to *listen* to what the horse is saying.

A very great horseman, possibly one imagines a nearly complete one, wrote this:

'The first great attribute of the horseman is humility, the second flexibility.'

He also wrote:

'We only begin to learn about horses when we begin to understand how much there is to learn.'

Ground exercises

As a start roll the head from side to side, then move the shoulders up and down and rotate them also. It all helps to relax the big neck muscles which are frequently tightened as a result of tension.

Suppling

Trunk Rotating
Stand with feet apart with arms raised to the front. Swing both round to the left and then to the right as far as they can go. Keep the hips and legs as still as possible. 10 times to each side.

Arm Circling
Circle each arm forward, up and back and down in one movement, 6 times each. Then circle both together, 6 times. Finally reverse the rotation in both instances.

Knee Bending
Cup the knee in the hands and bring it smoothly up to the chest, 8 times with each leg.

Raise the leg upwards to a convenient table, hold the knee and then bend down the head to touch it, 6 times with each leg.

Hamstring – Waist
From upright position slide down the hands as far down the left leg as you can, come upright and repeat to the right, 10 times.

Side-Flexing the Trunk
Feet apart, hands on hips. Bend to left and right alternately keeping the trunk upright, 8 times to each side.

Strength

Tummy Strengtheners
Lie on your back, arms outstretched behind the head. Keep knees slightly bent, sit up and reach for toes. Uncurl slowly, 5 times (8 as you get fitter).

Sit on a chair with legs outstretched. Raise legs until, after some practice, you can press your thighs to your chest. Return legs to ground slowly, 3 times at first, then try for 6.

Push-ups
Bend arms until chest touches table, then push up to start position, 8 times (when fit 15 is not too many).

Squats
Feet a little apart, hands on hips, bend knees and keep back straight. Straighten to stand on tip-toe, 5 times at first.

Stamina

Elbow to Knee
Sit cross-legged, hands clasped behind head. Bend to touch right knee with left elbow. Hold for 5 seconds and return slowly to start position. Repeat with left knee to right elbow. Once each way is probably enough.

Bench Steps
Use a stout stool or box about 30cm (12in) high. With left leg leading step up and step down briskly. Repeat with right leg leading. 15 steps each.

The Bow
Lie face down, bend knees and point toes. Raise chest and head, reach back and grasp the feet. Bring knees off floor and lift chin and chest. Do this slowly and do it just once.

Working on the lunge

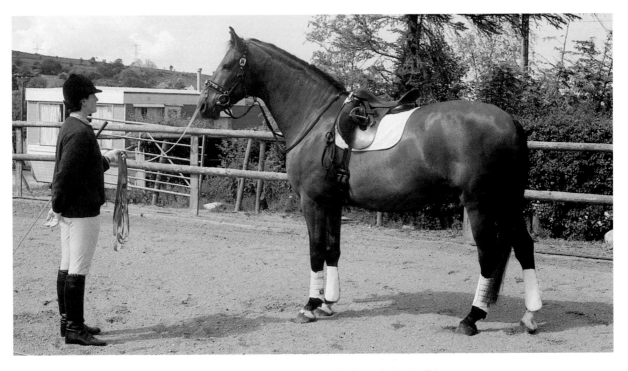

1. (Above): The lunge horse. The choice of a lunge horse is all-important.

2. (Below): Easy, comfortable paces and a temperament to match are necessary characteristics.

Exercises at halt

(Opposite):
3.
The first requirement is to obtain a good position at halt.

4–7
These are some of the leg exercises that will give confidence and encourage suppleness and balance whilst helping to deepen the seat.

4.

5.

6.

7.

Position – Position – Position

8.
Position established at halt. Note that the rider supports the position with the outside, right hand.

9.
Upright, deep and relaxed at walk.

10.
This position at trot is entirely commendable. (Note that in all these pictures the trainer is very clearly in command of the situation.)

11.
The next stage is for the rider to hold the hands in the riding position and to learn to do so at all three paces.

Exercises in movement

12.
Grasping the saddle fore and aft has the effect of pulling the seat down.

13.
Rotating the arm without twisting the waist does wonders for posture.

14.
Both arms circling at trot.

15.
Arms stretching from the chest.

16.
Not so easy as it looks. Arms swinging back to front at trot without loss of equilibrium.

Section 2

Chapter 6

The Paces

The three school paces are walk, trot, and canter and for the purposes of arena work these are further sub-divided. We shall now look at these in more detail and also consider the application of the halt.

The walk

Medium walk.

The four sub-divisions of walk are: *medium, collected, extended* and *free*. The walk is a pace of four separate beats made by the successive placing of each lateral pair of feet. The *sequence* when

the walk starts on the left leg is: left hind, left fore, right hind, right fore.

Collected walk with the base and outline shortened.

Medium walk is a free, active march movement showing moderate extension. The steps should be even and the four-beat rhythm quite distinct. The hindfeet touch the ground *in front* of the prints made by the forefeet.

Collected walk is the ultimate form of the walk pace and will not be attained until the horse is relatively advanced in his training. However, that must not prevent us from working steadily towards the goal of collection.

Collected walk is marked by a shortening of the outline as a result of the base itself being shortened. The horse is required to move resolutely forward with noticeable impulsion from the engaged hindlegs which are flexed strongly at the hocks. The head is held in a near vertical position with the neck raised and arched. The steps are necessarily shorter and more elevated than at medium walk because of the greater flexion of the joints. The hindfeet touch the ground *behind* the prints of the forefeet. In both instances the horse is required to be 'on the bit'.

(To be 'on the bit' the head is carried steadily with the face slightly in advance of the vertical. The horse is in light contact with the bit and accepts its presence and the rein tension without any sort of resistance. The horse is then termed as being submissive to the bit. It is a prerequisite for the hocks to be correctly placed, neither being carried to one side or the other in an attempted evasion. The neck is raised and arched and, very importantly, the poll is carried as its highest point. The degree to which the neck is raised depends on the stage of training and on the collection or extension of the pace.

The horse is 'behind the bit' when the neck is overbent and the nose inclined behind the vertical plane towards the chest. In that circumstance the highest point of the neck is about two-thirds along its length and behind the poll.

The horse is 'above the bit' when the nose is pointed upwards, above the rider's hand and as the highest point of the neck and head – a totally unacceptable position.)

Extended walk calls for the horse to cover as much ground as possible with each stride but without losing the regular four-beat pace. The head and neck are allowed to extend (indeed, they *must* extend) without the rider losing contact with the mouth and the hindfeet touch the ground *noticeably in advance* of the prints of the forefeet.

Free walk with the outline lowered and extended.

Free walk is a rest pace, the horse lowering and extending the outline with head and neck lowered and stretched out.

Application of the aids

To move into walk from halt, the aids are applied in the usual Prepare – Act – Yield sequence.

The horse is prepared by the momentary inward squeeze of both legs on the impulsion button, Point A, at the rear edge of the girth, and a simultaneous closure of the fingers. He has then to march forward directly to his front in response to the action of both legs applied in a smooth, inward, forward rolling motion, which is accompanied by the fingers relaxing to allow the requested movement forward.

Should the horse not respond to the leg aid, it must be supported by a quick, light 'tickle' with the whip. The object throughout should be to obtain a balanced, immediate response to increasingly light indications made by the legs.

It goes without saying that the smooth, active transition into walk and the subsequent movement in the pace will be impeded if the rider becomes stiff in the hips. The hips must lead the movement, if they become fixed the horse's action is at once restricted to a greater or lesser degree.

Importance of the walk

There is an old maxim that says a horse that walks well will gallop in a like manner, and that is usually true enough. Similarly, a good walk obtained by intelligent schooling in the early stages will, by and large, result in a good trot and canter. Of course, the quality of the three paces exhibited by an individual is subject to variation; some horses, as, for instance, the Welsh Cob/Thoroughbred crosses, are naturally impressive in trot and perhaps less so in canter. Nonetheless, a good, well-developed walk will improve the quality of both trot and canter. For that reason it is essential for riders to work on improving this basic pace.

Surprisingly, even though the imperfections of training are more apparent in the walk than otherwise, since it is more difficult to disguise weaknesses than in trot or canter, the walk is the most neglected of paces, and that stricture is often as applicable to the advanced horse as to those in the lower grades. Much of the problem is due to the rider's inability to exert the influence of developed muscles in the lower back and so to maintain the back's natural curve. Interestingly, the supreme exponent of the walk was Nuno Oliveira, who had an unusually strong and controlled back and produced horses that were supremely light in hand as a result.

To develop effective back aids takes time and application, but we can all avoid what is probably the most common failing in obtaining the good, free marching walk which is concerned with that most pernicious practice of imposing an outline before the horse is ready to conform to that shape.

The preoccupation with outline and the horse being 'on the bit' too often results in the walk being spoilt in all its divisions. In the early stages the horse should not be asked to walk 'on the bit' and still less should he be compelled to adopt a false outline by hands niggling away at the front end whilst the engagement of the hindlegs is neglected.

Nonetheless, once a good, free medium walk has been obtained and the horse goes forward energetically in the free and extended paces the work towards collection can begin. At the outset our efforts at shortening the horse will hardly be perceptible and certainly of no more than minimal duration. At first one must be satisfied with the horse taking a few strides in the shortened frame and then, in time, working in the outline, without resistance, for a few minutes before being rewarded with a pat and a short period of relaxation at extended walk.

The shortening and elevation is obtained from an active, medium walk by the rider increasing, tactfully, the driving aids of the back and seat which push *forward* and *upward* with each stride while the legs act on the impulsion button in intermittent squeezes. These actions result in greater engagement of the hindlegs and increased impulsion. If the hands then resist, again intermittently, by closing on the rein the energy generated will be contained within the framework imposed by the driving and restraining aids.

Of course, it will not happen unless the horse's back is free from stiffness and that in turn will depend, largely, upon the poll and jaw being flexed and supple. In theory there should be no difficulty, but in practice it can be just the reverse, with the horse thinking up all sorts of evasions to avoid working within the required frame.

Most commonly he can drop the bit, an action best countered by moving on strongly in the medium pace, or he may swing his quarters off the line so that the necessary engagement and impulsion is lost. Simplistically, this can be countered by the action of the single leg applied at Button B in a direct inward squeeze against the offending flank, but the lasting solution will be found when the horse is confirmed in the straightening exercises discussed in later sections.

Half-halt to halt

The fundamental riding requirement is contained in three

Square halt with horse on the bit.

Half-halt in trot with the hindleg well engaged, the horse making the initial response to the momentarily restraining hand.

The horse re-balanced and lightened in front as a result of the driving leg aid acting in conjunction with the restraining hand.

words Start – Steer – Stop and having got the horse under way it is now appropriate to consider the third element of the trio and to do so via the half-halt, which involves the aids acting in the preparatory role, as well as in the wider sense of re-imposing the balance within any pace. It results, when correctly applied, in the lightening of the forehand as a result of more actively engaged hindlegs and puts the horse in a posture from which he is better able to make the subsequent movement.

To make the half-halt the rider increases the influence of the back, seat and legs, the inside leg predominating (when riding on a circle) to drive the horse forward, even to the extent of bringing the shoulders slightly to the rear of the hips but *without rotating the pelvis*. Almost, but not quite simultaneously, the hands are raised by the veriest fraction and the fingers closed to prevent any increase in speed. As a result, the hindlegs are compelled to engage further under the body and, since the forehand has been subjected to the restraining lift of the hands, it will be raised and lightened.

The most usual fault is for the rider to be too strong in giving the aids. In perfection the whole operation should be almost imperceptible. A further danger lies in the hands being brought to the rear in a backward pull. To avoid this the rider has to think of them moving on an arc pivoting on the mouth, the action being upwards and forwards rather than otherwise and then descending smoothly on the same arc.

The half-halt is only as effective, however, as the response made to the legs. Unless the horse goes forward immediately from the leg, the second part of the operation, the raising and the closing hands, achieves nothing since it depends upon the movement from the leg.

If there is a failing in impulsion the action of the hands does nothing more than shorten the neck and force the back to hollow. There can be no question of re-balancing the body mass.

For the horse to benefit from the half-halt it needs to be practised continually during the schooling session, up to half a dozen times, indeed, for every circuit made of the arena – and that calls for a degree of concentration on the part of both horse and rider.

Halt

The half-halt prepares the horse for the full halt, which is a defined movement and, indeed, it may be preceded by a couple of discreet half-halts.

The halt is then no more than an extension of the latter, the intermittent restraining aids being applied a little more strongly until the horse stops. It is, however, important to keep the legs on the horse when the rein is relaxed (not 'given') so that the halt is made correctly. The legs may then be *relaxed* but not to the point where all pressure is removed. (It is absolutely essential for *intermittent* pressures to be observed. If the aid, of either hand or leg, is clamped on unremittingly, the horse is driven into resistance and there is no hope of achieving a smooth, balanced halt.)

The usual failing in a halt is for the horse to trail a hindleg, which can be felt from the saddle as that side will be lowered. To correct this, the rider squeezes forward from a little behind the girth with the leg on the side of the errant hindleg to bring it forward as a result of the contraction of the stomach muscles. A foreleg too far under the body can be corrected by easing the rein on that side and giving a little push with the corresponding leg.

If the horse halts badly it is never any good trying to correct him at that juncture; instead ride forward and try again.

If the horse has been accustomed to halting squarely in-hand and on the lunge and then confirmed in the half-halt, the halt itself should not be a difficulty.

The trot

As with the walk there are sub-divisions of the trot pace: *working, medium, collected* and *extended*.

The trot is a two-beat pace, the horse placing one pair of diagonal legs on the ground and springing, after a moment of suspension, on to the other diagonal. One beat is heard as the left hind and the right fore touch the ground simultaneously and the second, after the briefest interval, as the opposite diagonal touches the ground.

The trot is obtained from the walk, following the initial preparatory half-halt, by the closing of the legs, the yielding of the hand etc. as in the move-off into walk.

Working trot, active with good impulsion and engagement of the hindleg.

A vigorous, forward-going medium trot with the rider's leg placed in the driving position behind the girth.

Collected trot with elevation. (This horse has the natural elevation derived from his Welsh ancestry.)

Splendid engagement behind results in the lengthened stride of the extended trot.

Working trot, the most productive in this most valuable of the schooling paces, lies between *medium* and *collected*, being more inclined towards the latter than otherwise. It is seen as the approach to full collection. The hindfeet touch down a little behind the imprint of the forefeet.

Medium trot is between extension and collection, inclining towards the former. It is rounder than the extended pace but demands, nonetheless, good, active engagement of the hindlegs, the hindfeet touching down in the prints of the forefeet.

In *collected trot* the stride is shortened and becomes noticeably more elevated, the hindfeet falling behind the prints of the forefeet. The head is carried close to the vertical with the neck raised and arched.

The *extended trot* covers as much ground as possible with a *lengthened* stride – it is not a question of going faster! Maintaining the same rhythm, the steps are lengthened as a result of increased engagement behind in response to the active use of the leg. The horse remains 'on the bit' but the hands allow the neck to lower and extend so as to prevent the action being elevated.

The extremes in the trot spectrum are represented by *collection* and *extension*. *Working* trot is positioned slightly to the collected side of the centre line, whilst *medium* trot comes closer to the extension.

The most common failing in trot is to go too fast. It is more productive to slow the pace so as to obtain more impulsion and maintain a steady rhythm.

When riding at trot the rider may either rise (or post) or sit. In the first instance the seat is raised *slightly* out of the saddle on alternate beats, a light contact being maintained by the crotch which makes up the third element of the 3-point seat.

At sitting trot, it is essential for the hips to remain flexible and the trunk upright, the open seat absorbing the shock through a supple, naturally curved back that *undulates* with the movement of the horse. The critical portion is the small of the back and its accompanying musculature which is the connecting link between the trunk and the lower body.

The ability to sit easily at trot is an essential accomplishment in schooling the horse but it is best practised sparingly in the early stages of training when the horse's back structure is still undeveloped and he has yet to obtain a roundness in the top-line. If sitting trot is executed heavily and the rider's back is insufficiently supple, a situation often accompanied by fixed or even retreating hips, then it will do more harm than good. Should the horse stiffen at sitting trot it is very advisable to ride on briskly at rising trot so as to ease the back.

(Rising trot is still referred to as 'posting'. The origin lies in the practice evolved by the *post*-boys of the seventeenth and eighteenth centuries to mitigate the discomfort caused by the jarring paces of the rough animals which were their usual lot. In India, curiously, it is termed 'bumping' trot – which is just what it should not be!)

When rising at the trot in the execution of the circle there remains the question of 'changing the diagonal'. It is generally accepted that the rational practice is to sit on the inside diagonal, that is when the inside fore and outside hind are on the ground. (On the circle left the inside diagonal is the left fore and right hind and vice versa.)

The reason for doing so is that it is easier, and more effective, to apply the inside leg to engage the corresponding hindleg of the horse when the seat is in the saddle rather than out of it.

Changes of diagonal, even on what seems a straight line or when out hacking, are very necessary if we are not to cause one-sided muscular development of the horse's back by always riding on the same diagonal. The rider should, in a short time, be able to feel which diagonal they are using, but it can always be confirmed by a quick downwards glance at the shoulders.

The canter

The sub-divisions at canter are: *collected, working, medium* and *extended*.

The pace is one of three distinct beats and the horse may lead with either the left fore (for the circle left) or the right fore (for circle right). In fact, however, the sequence of footfalls in canter to the right, for instance, is left hindleg, then simultaneously, the legs of the left diagonal, i.e. left fore and right hind, and finally the leading leg, the right fore. This is followed by a period of suspension before the next stride is taken.

Collected canter requires the horse to move forward 'on the bit' and with the head raised and the neck arched. The quarters are well engaged and there is a noticeable lightness of the forehand. The strides are shorter than in the other variations of the pace but the horse is more mobile and the movement altogether lighter.

Working canter lies between collected and medium.

Medium canter lies between working and extended canter. In this pace the stride is reasonably extended and there must be an evident thrust from the quarters. The horse is 'on the bit' but carries the head a little in front of the vertical with the head and neck being a shade lower in consequence – lower, that is, than at working canter and lower again than in the collected pace.

Collected canter in good overall balance and a slightly shortened outline

A very free-working canter, the pace between collected and medium.

Medium canter. The stride is reasonably extended.

Extended canter immediately before the head is lowered and the foreleg extended, but showing powerful engagement of the quarters. (For once, the rider has momentarily lost her exemplary leg position.)

Counter canter with the horse bent towards the leading leg whilst maintaining excellent balance.

The moment of suspension in the canter pace.

In *extended canter* the stride covers as much ground as possible as a result of strong impulsion in the quarters. Remaining 'on the bit' the horse lowers and stretches out the head and neck, the face being in front of the vertical.

Counter canter is when the horse is asked to canter a left-handed circle on the right lead or vice versa. He is accordingly bent towards the leading leg. This is a suppling movement and is performed as a balancing exercise as well as featuring in more advanced level dressage tests.

If the horse, in contravention of his rider's aids, leads with the 'wrong leg' it is termed a 'false' lead.

To obtain a smooth canter depart from trot the rider can make use of the corner of the school since it encourages the horse in the correct bend.

The horse is ridden actively into the corner at sitting trot, following the preparatory half-halt. The rider stretches the inside leg to weight the corresponding seat bone, places the holding outside leg flat against the horse on Button B and acts with the driving inside leg on Button A. Meanwhile the inside rein, supported by the outside, can be raised and opened (moved outward) fractionally. (If the inside rein is used as a rein of opposition – see 'rein effect' p. 35 – the quarters swing outwards and interference is caused to the first canter stride. The outside leg, supporting its partner, discourages any evasion of the quarters to the outside.)

Additionally, since the horse at canter will carry the inside shoulder and hip in advance of the opposite ones, the rider has to conform to the movement by advancing the corresponding seat bone.

Common faults contributing to faulty canter strike-offs are concerned with the rider being out of balance, collapsing the hip, leaning forward, inclining the trunk away from the movement and so on. The hands may also prevent a smooth departure into the pace by failing to yield sufficiently or quickly enough and so restricting the action of the leading leg.

A common fault. The horse is on the forehand at canter because of the rider's imbalance (intentional in this instance).

Section 3

Chapter 7

School Figures and Movements

Many people say, that all things
in the Manège are nothing but
Tricks, and Dancing, and Gambolls,
and of no use: But by their Leave,
whoever says so is very much
Deceived . . .
  Wm Cavendish, Duke of Newcastle (1592–1676)

The contribution to the understanding of equitation made by Newcastle is probably insufficiently recognised. He was, however, the first and perhaps the only English Master and his work was both accepted and acclaimed by his European contemporaries. (The quaint punctuation and use of capitals in the quote from *La Méthode et Invention Nouvelle de Dresser les Chevaux* cannot be attributed wholly to His Grace. Punctuation was in its formative stages in his time and the rash of commas is probably the work of subsequent editors.)

The figures performed within the arena are the equivalent of the rider's physical exercises, increasing the strength and suppleness of the horse certainly, but also contributing to the overall balance and straightness.

Straightness

Straightness is the final element in the three commandments handed down to us by the classical masters and so succinctly expressed by one of France's greatest horsemen, General L'Hotte.

L'Hotte's uncompromising dictum encompassing the very roots of equestrian endeavour was this:

CALM – FORWARD – STRAIGHT

In those three words are contained all the principles of schooling.

Calm in the horse is a pre-requisite. Without it the horse is inattentive, unresponsive and almost certainly disobedient. When the horse is calm he can be taught to go *forward*. Going forward from the impulsion created in the quarters and virtually in front of the action of the rider's legs is not a matter of just moving to the front. It is a definite urge displayed by the horse and is just as much a mental quality as a physical manifestation.

For a horse to be *straight*, the hindfeet must be able to follow exactly in the track made by the forefeet. When that happens we have optimum efficiency of the mechanical structure, since the hindlegs deliver their propulsive thrust directly to the front without it being partially expended by being directed to one side or the other. It follows that when the horse is straight the rider has reached the point where they are in control of the quarters, and it is the quarters that control the horse. (As a simple example, horses refuse at fences when they cease to *go forward* from the rider's legs. When they run out at a fence they use the quarters, the origin of directional movement, to frustrate the rider's intentions. In theory, and so long as the horse is not overfaced, refusals are nigh on impossible in the horse that has learnt to go forward and is straight, the position of his quarters being under the control of the rider's legs.)

However, straightness is rather more involved than that. It is a prime consideration in training and we seek to achieve it through exercises like shoulder-in, for instance. But before we can reach that point, and after, we need to be constantly concerned with straightening the horse in every stage of the school exercises. For that reason we need to have a general appreciation of what constitutes crookedness and of the techniques employed to eliminate it.

In almost every instance the problem is with the off-hind. Most horses have difficulty in engaging and flexing that leg in comparison with its partner and they may often put the foot down outside and thus to the right of the track made by the corresponding forefoot. (The problem will be exacerbated if the rider sits out of balance and is heavy in the use of the seat bones.) The resulting stiff side, and all horses have a 'stiff' or stiffer side, causes the horse to lean on the opposite rein and against the rider's leg on that side.

There is no point in trying to force the horse into bending that stiff side. He will only respond with an increased resistance because of the discomfort he experiences. Nor is it any use trying to correct the situation at halt or walk. One has to work at a good active trot, giving and taking with the rein on the stiff

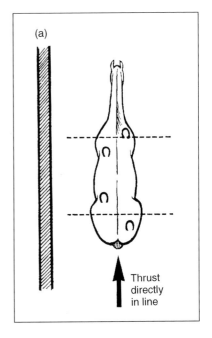

The Straight Horse
Figure a shows the thrust from the quarters delivered directly in line with the track made by the forefeet.

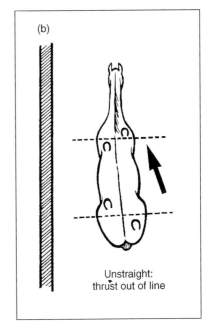

Figure b shows the quarters carried outside the track of the forefeet, thus detracting from the propulsive thrust and stiffening the movement.

side, the hand acting as though it were squeezing a rubber ball. The opposite rein is held in support, whilst the right leg is active in asking for engagement of the off-hind.

Work on circles and turns, opening the stiff rein and directing it towards the hip, and then ride circles with the hands in even contact so that the horse describes the circle in the *wrong* bend. This is uncomfortable for the horse and should not therefore be overdone, but because it is uncomfortable he will, after only a few circles, slowly begin to give on the stiff side and accept the outside rein. (Do not imagine that this is unorthodox, it has been practised and understood for 400 years or more.)

In the school figures the horse can be straightened after passing through the corners if his shoulder is kept away from the wall or the outside of the arena. It is done by moving the inside hand a little to the side and laying the outside rein lightly on the neck, almost in the manner of the fourth rein effect.

The school figures and exercises are based on the horse working on circles and elements of circles and they include calling for transitions and the variations within a single pace which will improve the longitudinal suppleness of the horse. By that is meant the ability to lengthen and to shorten the outline and the base in response to driving aids creating impulsion which is either contained by the light, intermittent action of the hand, to produce shortening, or released to produce lengthening. It is the work on the circle that leads ultimately to the *straight* horse.

The lunge work on either rein in the early stages of training act as a preparation for riding the school figures. Lateral suppling is achieved by the stretching of the muscles on the outside of the body whilst those on the inside of the turn are contracted. The weight of the rider, however, presents an additional problem for the horse and although the trot is the most rewarding and suitable pace for the riding of these figures it should be preceded by some work at walk to accustom the horse to the pattern of these new exercises. (The trot compels full and even utilisation of the body, more so than either walk or canter. It is also easier for the horse to bend at this pace and then to straighten.)

The first of the school figures to be ridden is a full circuit of the *manège*. This will involve the execution of four quarter *voltes*, one at each corner of the arena. A *volte* is a small circle of determined size, a *circle* proper being of any size larger than that.

Academically, the radius of the volte is equal to the length of the horse. Taking that to be on average around 3m (10ft), then the radius of the volte is the same and the diameter will be 6m (20ft). To ride so small a circle in level balance (i.e. without the horse leaning over towards the centre) is *very* difficult and is by no means within the capability of horses in the secondary stage of schooling (nor, all too frequently, of riders who have yet to learn how to sit lightly in balance).

The quarter voltes are clearly less difficult, but they still require the horse to move on a 6m (20ft) bend and that too is well beyond a horse at this stage of training who will almost certainly be compelled to swing his quarters outwards.

It is easier for the horse if the corners are made rounder, so that the bend is the equivalent of a much larger circle of, say, 15m (50ft). He should then be able to follow the track of the forefeet with the hindlegs.

Corners should be thought of and ridden as elements of a circle, which is what they are, and not as distinct left or right *turns*.

Following the full circuits of the arena, we can ask for simple changes of rein, the circles to either hand, the figure-of-eight using 20m (66ft) circles, and after those the changes through the circle and simple serpentines.

The longitudinal suppling exercises also begin on the full circuit of the *manège* and though they are simple enough they too have to be approached with care, since they involve shortened strides at sitting trot. If they are introduced too early in the training programme when the horse is insufficiently muscled up there is a danger of his being driven into resistance, stiffening his back to avoid the discomfort he experiences. These exercises are, therefore, best left until the young horse has had an opportunity to build up his back muscles.

The easiest exercise is to shorten the stride at the ends of the arena. The reverse exercise, shortening down the long side, is more difficult and it is only when the horse is absolutely comfortable in both these figures that one should attempt the 20m (66ft) circles and the change of hand which forms a figure of eight. (In an arena measuring 20m (66ft) x 40m (131ft), two 20m (66ft) circles can be accommodated. In fact, of course, the horse describes something nearer to a 19m (62ft) circle since he has to work about half a metre from the wall.) Circles smaller than 20m (66ft) should not be attempted in trot until the horse has reached a more advanced stage of training and is in level balance.

To start riding 10m (33ft) circles too early puts so much strain on the horse that he is likely to resist the bend by 'falling' either in or out, that is he evades by carrying his quarters inside the track of the forefeet in the first instance and outside in the second. Either of these two failings is a sure indication that the horse is not ready for the exercise and is insufficiently supple to perform them adequately. The answer lies not in persisting but

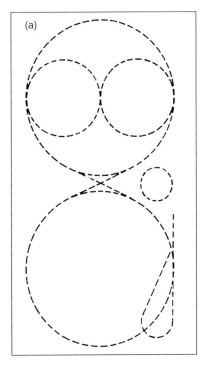

A selection of school figures. Figure a shows the circles and the changes of hand (direction), figure b indicates further possible changes of hand within the school area. The inside dotted line represents the 'inside' track, 2 metres (6.6ft) from the wall.

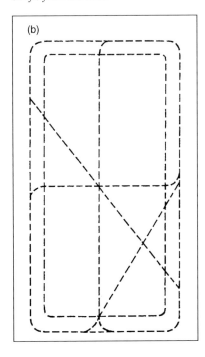

(Below and Pages 85-6):
Exercises in pace variation in trot and
canter. They are relatively difficult and
should not be attempted until the horse
is well-established in his school work.

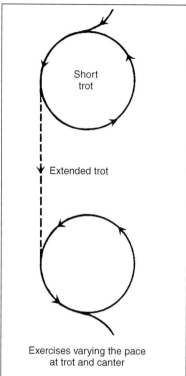

Exercises varying the pace
at trot and canter

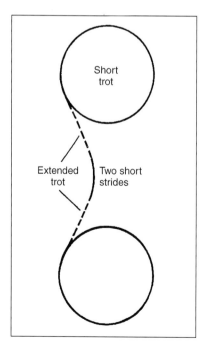

in going back to the general strengthening process, which will be realised by intelligently planned hacking sessions and by working on the lunge without the weight of the rider to inhibit either movement or balance.

(It is important to ensure that the arena markers are placed at the correct distances so that the rider is helped in riding accurately from one point to another. It is also helpful if circles can be marked with sawdust or something similar so as to familiarise riders with the sizes – 20m (66ft) circles can all too easily take on an undesirable ovoid character.)

Movements and Paces

The school figures seek to bring about a refinement in the paces by improving the response to the aids, the rhythm, impulsion and balance. The movements themselves increase the suppleness, straightness and balanced outline of the horse and will for the most part have a practical application. Whilst everything depends upon the horse's urge to go forward it is, after all, very useful in everyday riding if he has learnt how to take a few steps backwards and sideways as well as turning easily on both his forehand and quarters.

Before beginning to work seriously on the circles it is essential to have the horse *moving forward* willingly and with sufficient energy to make it necessary to exert just a modicum of restraint. Additionally, we have to demand, increasingly, an improvement in the *rhythm*, and that will not come about until the horse accepts a steady, equal and very light contact with the hands.

This will remain a prime consideration throughout the horse's training but until we see signs of it being realised there is no point in working on more advanced figures and movements which may well make it more difficult to establish the basic requirements. Most horses will sometimes give the feeling of holding back rather than making an immediate response to the legs. It may be an attempt to assert themselves. It can arise as a result of irritation or resentment, or out of plain old-fashioned laziness. If the horse is stiff from overwork or because of some physical weakness he will certainly be reluctant to comply with the requests being made of him. That situation should not arise if we are observant and careful in our management of the horse. If it does the horse has to be rested and put on a lighter work programme, with all the loss of time and continuity that entails.

Otherwise, we have to take action to correct the failing. We dare not allow the horse to get into the habit of disregarding the aids and as the schooling progresses we have to be ever more demanding in that respect, although we have to be certain that the horse's back muscles are sufficiently strong to allow an early response on his part.

If there is no answer to the leg aid, or if the response is delayed, do not repeat the aid but use the whip in a tickle or even a couple of firm taps behind the leg. If that fails then the spur must be brought into play, but only sufficiently to make him aware of its presence. By employing the aids in this sequence, each being a degree more imperative, but hardly more severe than the preceding one, we can in time obtain a more instant response to an ever lighter leg aid.

With the lazy horse there is a greater degree of difficulty. The temptation is to wake him up with a sharp cut of the whip or by a stronger application of the spurs. It may work in some instances, but we run the risk of the horse becoming resentful, particularly in respect of the spurs. Resentment of the latter can just as easily become habitual as disobedience and that could place a serious limitation on the horse's future performance. (In fact, until the rider can carry the leg still and steady, spurs are best avoided.)

There is, of course, no cut-and-dried answer. It all comes down to the individual horse and how developed is the 'feel' of the rider.

A skilful positive teacher may get over the problem from the ground by working both horse and rider through the medium of the voice and, if it is not too pie-in-the-sky, the projection of personality supported, ever so tactfully, by the material presence of a lunge whip.

Without doubt, there has to be a more demanding use of the aids. Many lazy horses respond to a slap down the shoulder with the long whip combined with a sharp click of the tongue. In other cases, an increase in the energy content of the food ration will be helpful. Again there can be no more than a rule-of-thumb guide, but if the heating element is increased until the horse is a little too bright for comfort – a condition best and more safely ascertained by his behaviour on the lunge – it can then be reduced to produce a more acceptable level of energy. Far more lazy horses than one would imagine could, indeed, be made more forward-going as a result of an increase in their ration of energising foods than by the more positive but potentially counter-productive application of legs, whip and spur.

Another practical, if less than purist solution, to the lazy horse, so long as you are well attuned to the character of your pupil, is to take the reins in one hand allowing them to loop a little; the legs are then applied and almost simultaneously one delivers a sharp reminder with the whip with the free hand and behind the leg. The horse will most probably bound forward, hence the need for that looping rein, but he may well have learnt his lesson.

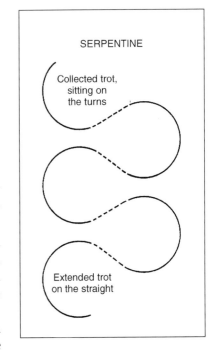

SERPENTINE

Collected trot, sitting on the turns

Extended trot on the straight

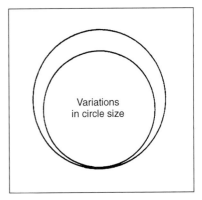

Variations in circle size

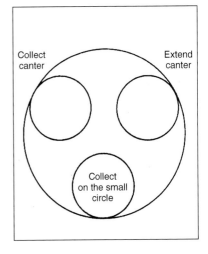

Collect canter

Extend canter

Collect on the small circle

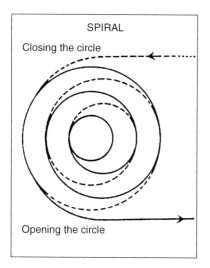

SPIRAL

Closing the circle

Opening the circle

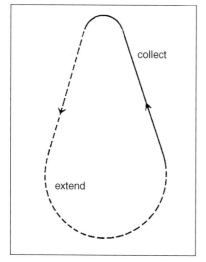

collect

extend

The object is to produce forward movement *with enthusiasm;* it is not sufficient for the horse to go forward in a quiet lack-lustre style. The ideal is for the horse to go forward energetically enough for the rider to need to apply a little restraint.

Thereafter, the aim is to establish a steady regular *rhythm* in the paces. In plain words we shall seek to maintain the correct order of the footfalls in each pace – four distinct, equally spaced beats at walk, two at trot, three at canter.

The flow from one step to the next is smooth and the regularity of the beat even. Both rider and horse will benefit if the schooling sessions can be accompanied by some judiciously chosen music. Modern recorders are so small that they can easily be carried by the rider if outside assistance is not available.

The essence of rhythmical movement is in going no faster – in fact just a shade slower – than the speed at which the horse can maintain his balance. If the horse is pushed into going above the speed at which he is comfortable the quality of the pace deteriorates and the strides become shorter and more hurried.

Inherent to rhythmical movement is the contact between bit and hands. The principle involved is concerned with the legs pushing the horse forward whilst the hands gradually take up a level contact. The horse has then to work within the frame dictated by the legs at one end and hands at the other. The frame, however, cannot and must not be rigid for that would imply constriction and restriction. At all times the hands follow the movement of the head, maintaining the contact even, and particularly, when the horse seeks to evade it by shortening his neck, retracting the nose, opening the mouth and so on. The horse then begins to learn and accept that contact is constant, unescapable and even comforting.

Whatever happens, contact must not be maintained by the hands moving back to pull. If the horse reduces, by one means or another, the degree of contact, he has to be made to retake it by the rider's leg pushing him forward more energetically, whilst not allowing any increase in the speed of the pace.

The circles

The introduction to the circle is the quarter *volte* which has to be performed in describing the full circuit of the arena.

When riding on a straight line it is comparatively easy to keep the horse in level balance. Changes of direction, however, be they ever so gradual, upset the balance. This imbalance results in a loss of impulsion, and an interruption to the rhythm of the pace.

The secret in riding the quarter *volte* and therefore when

The straight horse correctly bent on the circle 'round the rider's inside leg'.

entering the whole circle is to create more impulsion – that is, the energy created in the hindlegs and controlled and directed by the hands. It involves an increased use of the legs combined with a slightly firmer contact but no increase in speed. As the curve is entered emphasis is given to the inside leg, the inside rein is opened slightly by the hand moving outwards and the outside rein is lengthened by the advance of the outside hand, elbow and shoulder *and* the outside hip.

The philosophy is that of riding from the inside leg to the outside hand and is one which necessitates the rejection of some pretty sacred cows.

Deeply entrenched by continual repetition, both in the written word and in actual instruction, is the time-honoured formula relating to the changes of direction.

The instruction too often given is for the rider to *act* with the inside rein, supporting it with the outside hand and it is just not sufficiently clear. Action then usually entails the use of the *direct rein of opposition*, the third rein effect. *Support* should mean that the outside rein cedes, or is 'given', to allow the inside bend. I suspect, however, that in reality 'support' means just that: the acting hand operating against a base provided by the outside supporting hand and thus restricting the movements quite hopelessly.

The manuals having, it is true, urged the use of the inside leg to provide impulsion, ask for the outside (*supporting*) leg to act behind the girth so as to prevent the quarters swinging out and off the track of the forefeet.

The truth is that it is the opposing action of the direct rein which causes the quarters to swing outwards. Hand and leg are therefore at cross-purposes, the action of the former being opposed by the latter. The hand has created an unwanted movement which the leg seeks to rectify. It is hardly logical and is surely an unnecessary difficulty for both horse and rider.

To a degree it is probable that even with the employment of the opening rein the quarters will tend to shift a little to the outside and that movement will need to be countered by the outside leg, but there is no need to exaggerate the problem by an incorrect and restrictive use of the rein. Indeed, it makes no sense at all, and with that the horse would probably agree!

Turn on the forehand

This is a basic movement learnt in the stable when the horse was taught to 'move over' and there should be no difficulty in teaching him to move his quarters round the pivot of his forehand from the saddle, although the turn on the forehand is not natural to the horse. Very occasionally a startled horse at liberty may perform something approaching a turn on the quarters, when the forehand turns round the pivot provided by the latter, but never will he turn on his forehand. The natural way for the horse to turn is on his centre when he moves his four legs round the vertical axis at the girth.

Nonetheless, in the schooling of the horse this unnatural turn is of enormous importance. Indeed, the turns on the forehand and quarters mark the watershed between the partially schooled horse and the trained one.

The reasons for teaching this turn are as follows:

(1) When the horse moves his quarters either to the left or the right in response to the action of a single leg he is compelled to lift and cross the hindlegs. It is, therefore, possible to supple and strengthen each hindleg individually, improving the joint flexion and also increasing the power of the all-important loin on which all movement must be based.

(2) Once the rider has the ability to move the quarters at will it follows that he is also able to prevent any *unwanted* shift. He is, therefore, by being in control of the quarters, equipped to *straighten* his horse.

(3) The turn which gives us mobility of the quarters also gives us mobility of the jaw, and thus the ability to obtain flexion on either side of the mouth. (There is therefore a beneficial influence extending through the horse from the mouth to

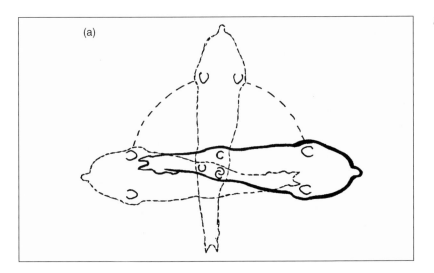

a. Turn on the Forehand.

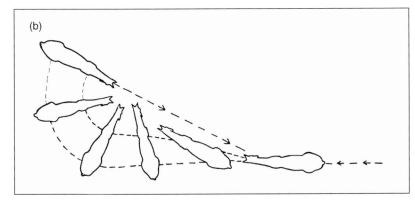

b. The turn approached from the reverse half-volte.

(Below):
In this 'un-natural' turn the horse is asked to move the quarters round the forelegs. The movement teaches mobility of the quarters and enables the rider to control their position.

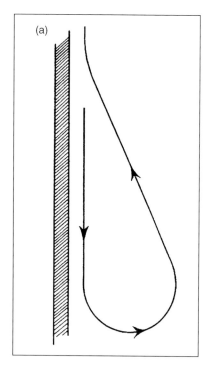

a. Is the half-volte from which the turn on the quarters can be approached.

b. Is the reversed half-volte used to teach the opposite turn on the forehand.

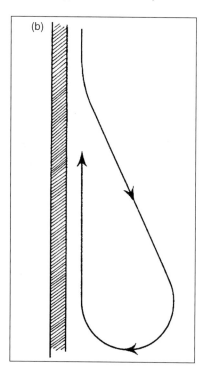

the loins and hindlegs.)

(4) It represents the initial introduction to lateral work.

(5) It is quite impossible on a very prosaic level to open a gate with any degree of competence unless the horse is capable of performing a turn on the forehand.

As a start the horse can be taught to shift his quarters from a tapping whip applied behind the girth whilst the trainer stands at his head. Within two days one should be able to walk the horse forward (for the turn is just as much concerned with forward movement as anything else), the trainer necessarily walking backwards and leading him from his bridle. One then checks the horse and moves the quarters over with a touch of the whip. It is, of course, essential to practise the movement in both directions. When the horse is ready to attempt the turn under saddle the rider needs to be very clear in his mind about the aids he is going to apply. An incorrect combination of rein and leg will confuse the horse, whilst any contradictory requests made through the aids will very effectively prohibit the execution of the movement.

The turn can be approached from walk, the horse being checked (half-halt) before being brought to halt. If the quarters are to be moved to the right the left leg is placed flat behind the girth (position B) and is pushed inwards. (Avoid at all costs the digging heel and turned out toe which might disturb the horse's composure.) The right leg is held ready in case it is necessary to limit any excessive movement.

In concert with the left leg we use the left rein in the fifth effect, that is the indirect rein of opposition (to the haunches) behind the withers, placing the rein (without pulling backwards) carefully towards the right hip, whilst easing the right rein to permit the head to turn slightly to the left. Both hand and leg act simultaneously and intermittently. The intermittent use of the aids is far more persuasive than an unbroken pressure and less likely to disturb the horse.

To increase the mobility and to carry the horse a stage further (though 180°) the turn can be practised from the *reversed half volte*, a ponderous title for a very simple movement. It involves riding off the track and returning to it and, therefore, turning about by means of a 6m (20ft) circle. As the circle is entered the same aids are applied, following a slight half-halt, and the horse takes his quarters round his forehand to return to the track. The usual rider problem is to increase the measure of the aids rather than doing otherwise, a practice that results in tension and stiffness and creates quite unnecessary difficulties in the execution of a simple movement.

The leg-yielding exercise moving the horse from the inside track outwards to the rails.

Leg-yielding

This is the first of the lateral suppling exercises and the obvious follow on from the forehand turn. It imposes no strain on the horse and is very easy for him to perform, since we are not asking that he should bend his body.

The horse is accustomed to the lateral aids which have been applied in the forehand turn. The same aids are now applied to move the whole body to the side away from the pressure of the rider's leg.

The exercise begins in walk and we should take advantage of the inside track, that is a track some 2m (6ft) inside the perimeter of the arena and parallel to it. Put on this new circuit, the horse, being a creature of habit and always happy to return to the familiar, will be willing and even anxious to move outward in order to take up the original track.

With the horse moving in an active walk the lateral aids are applied on the long sides to move the horse sideways onto the track. If we are moving to the left (right leg, right indirect rein of opposition) the supporting hand (the left one) is carried slightly outwards to emphasis the direction in which we want the horse to move. Additionally it supports the right rein by preventing the bit from being pulled through the mouth and it checks any tendency for the neck to be bent more than a shade to the right. Only a *slight* flexion to the right is needed. We use the left leg to maintain the impulsion and, if necessary, to control any excess movement.

Leg-yielding can not only be practised in the schooling arena, but also on the lanes when out hacking, the horse being moved into and away from the side of the roadway.

Within a week or so the horse should be able to yield in either direction from trot and to do so without interrupting the rhythm.

The only real difficulties that may occur in the leg-yielding exercise are those which may arise because of the rider exaggerating the movement and producing a sort of false shoulder-in with far too much bend in the neck.

For this reason do not attempt the leg-yielding exercise on the outside track when it is only possible to produce a travesty of the shoulder-in.

Shoulder-in

This exercise, first practised by the eighteenth-century French Master de la Guérinière, has been described as the ultimate

Right shoulder-in made from the circle

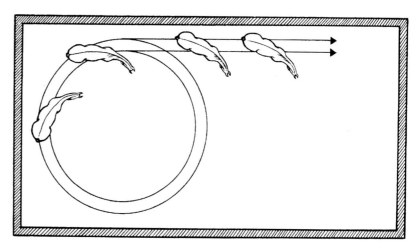

supling exercise. It is certainly that, but also, once perfected, it gives the rider a very high degree of control over the horse and leads to both straightness and collection. It is valueless if it is done incorrectly, so the rider must understand what the shoulder-in seeks to accomplish and then be absolutely clear about the execution of the exercise.

The ideal is for the horse to be 'bent' round the inside leg of the rider, the quarters square in relation to the wall and moving parallel to it. The hips, therefore, are virtually at right angles to the wall. The head and neck are to be inclined

Left shoulder-in with the quarters square in relation to the rail and the movement led by the outside shoulder.

Common Faults: A. Insufficient bend. B. Head bent excessively to the inside.

A.

B.

slightly away from the movement, which is led by the outside shoulder. The inside foreleg passes and crosses in front of the outside leg and the inside hindleg is placed in front of the outside.

That is the official definition of the FEI and can hardly be bettered, although it is not possible to 'bend' the horse round the inside leg – if by that one is suggesting that there is a bend in the spine. That is just not possible, since the spine, except for some minimal movement in the dorsal vertebrae, is a rigid structure. What is meant is that the horse in making the turn gives the impression of being bent round the leg by the muscles on the inside being flattened whilst those of the opposite side are stretched and assume a greater prominence.

The shoulder-in becomes a path leading to collection because of the increased engagement of the inside hindleg under the body. This is facilitated by the increased freedom of the diagonal partner, the outside foreleg, as a result of the shoulder being 'opened' by the inward inclination of the neck and head. Furthermore, if the position is correct, the inside hip has to be lowered and that in itself contributes to a greater engagement of the leg and, of course, an increase in the flexion of the leg's three joints.

The classical shoulder-in is, in the opinion of some authorities, a movement on three tracks. However, it can be on four tracks and still be correct. It all depends on the degree of the bend.

Shoulder-in is most easily ridden off a circle, so if we approach the exercise from a 20m (66ft) circle with the horse correctly bent to correspond with a circle of that diameter, the curve will be too shallow to produce a three-track movement. If the quarters are held square, as they should be, the movement will be on four overlapping tracks. A little more bend on a 10m (33ft) circle will result in a three-track movement but we cannot expect that until the horse is sufficiently supple to comply.

The advanced horse, who can be ridden through the corners on a true quarter *volte,* that is on a 6m (20ft) bend, will produce a four-track movement as a result, so long as the 6m (20ft) bend is held as it should be.

In both instances it is only the forelegs which are actually crossed.

Unhappily this is not always understood and one frequently sees riders deliberately attempting to produce a movement in which both legs cross and in which the quarters are not as a result held square. That is not shoulder-in. If it is anything it is a kind of exaggerated leg-yielding and is of no gymnastic value.

The pace for shoulder-in is the trot, in which greater impulsion can be obtained, but initially the movement is best attempted from walk, which is easier for both horse and rider and is less likely to be confusing.

To begin, ride a 20m (66ft) circle. It will, in fact, be about 19m (62ft) and if it can be reduced comfortably to 18m (59ft) that will be even better. However, it must be a very good circle and the rider has to ride positively from an active inside leg to the outside hand. When it is established we can begin shoulder-in between the quarter and half markers. The optimum moment is when the quarters are in line with the quarter marker and the horse is bent to continue on the circle.

In fact, it can be said to begin a stride or so before that when the head is in line with the marker. At that point we demand the horse's attention by a light half-halt and then, in simple terms, we ask the horse to move down the long side whilst the bend is maintained.

When the horse can execute the movement easily at walk *and to both left and right* the shoulder-in can be ridden from trot to the point when it can be approached from a 15m (49ft) or, better still, a 10m (33ft) circle, although the latter cannot be expected until the horse is pretty well confirmed in the school work and is well-muscled and supple.

Aids for shoulder-in

The inside leg acts actively on the girth in the prescribed rear–front motion to push the outside shoulder along the track. The outside leg is held flat behind the girth (position B) to stop any twisting or falling-out of the quarters. However should there be any failing in impulsion it must be used in a driving role to reinforce its partner.

The rider's weight is concentrated more on the inside seat bone than otherwise, by the leg being stretched and the foot pressed on the stirrup. This shift of the balance to the inside accords with the horse's position and encourages the sideways movement.

The inside rein acts behind the withers in the fifth rein effect, whilst the outside rein opens slightly to indicate the required direction in the initial steps. Thereafter it acts to support its partner in holding the bend in the neck. Both hands have to be carried to the outside *without* the inner hand crossing the withers.

The temptation is to lead the movement with the outside hip and to allow the inside leg to act behind rather than on the girth on the 'impulsion button'. That will only result in the quarters moving out of their square position and becoming twisted. The rider has, instead, to keep his hips aligned to those of the horse *but* his shoulders must turn to the *inside* to follow the movement and remain in parallel to those of the horse.

This is a paramount consideration and it emphasises the need to have a full understanding of the movement, the rein aids and the positioning of the body in relation to that of the horse. The rider has to conform to the movement of the horse in relation, particularly, to hips and shoulders. Secondly, he must ride with his mind as well as his body.

If the horse should display hesitancy in his progress down the long side in the shoulder-in position he can be helped by the inside rein being laid on his neck and used in a raising, slightly pushing movement in time with the lifting, sideways placement of the inside foreleg.

The shoulder-in position is maintained for the strides between the point of departure from the circle and the corresponding point between the half- and quarter-markers at the further end of the long side, when the horse, in the same bend, resumes the circle at the opposite end of the arena.

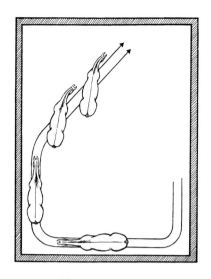

The progression into half-pass to the right.

From left to right: shoulder-in, travers and renvers.

Travers – Renvers – Half-Pass

It is possible to teach the half-pass, an uncompromising four-track movement, from the shoulder-in, but it is far more easily approached from the exercise known as *travers*, which is also called *head-to-the-wall* or *quarters-in* and is another four-track movement.

Once more it is approached from the circle but now the bend is towards the movement. It begins at the moment the neck and shoulders become virtually parallel to the wall, the exact opposite of the shoulder-in movement. The forehand then proceeds directly on the track, the quarters are bent inwards and the hindlegs cross.

The rider holds this bend and maintains the forward movement by the inside leg acting on the girth as in the shoulder-in.

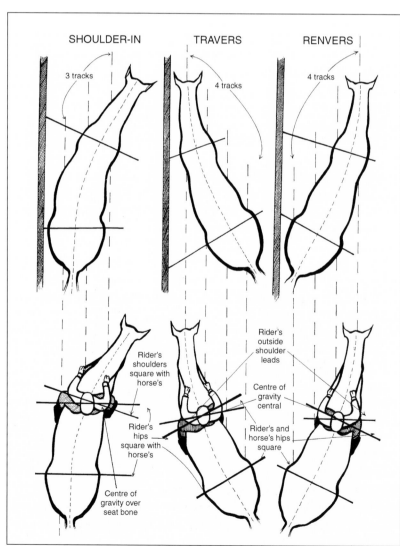

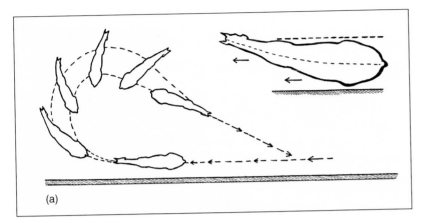

a. Half-turn on the quarters approached from the half-volte.

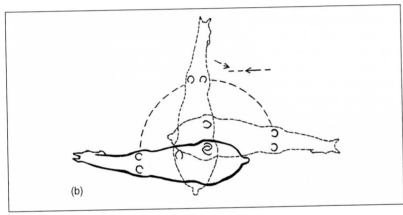

b. Detail of the half-turn.

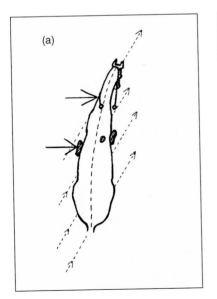
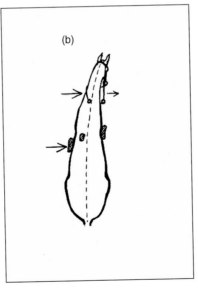

Application of aids for:
a. Half-pass; b. Turn on the quarters;

The hands are carried to the inside without the outside one crossing the withers. The outside hand predominates and acts in conjunction with the inside leg. The rider's outside shoulder is well forward but the seat is otherwise held centrally.

c. Turn on the forehand;
d. Leg-yielding.

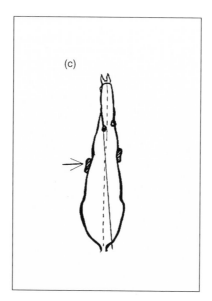

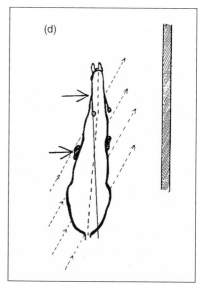

Travers from the rear with the horse advancing on four tracks.

The travers position seen from the front.

Half-pass to the left, the horse correctly positioned immediately before the outside leg crosses the inner.

Renvers, *tail-to-the-wall* or *quarters-out* is the reverse movement and in this the horse becomes independent of the guiding wall.

In *half-pass* the horse moves obliquely forward, slightly bent round the rider's inside leg and with the head inclined towards the direction of the movement. It is approached from the circle and the object is to move forwards and sideways with the horse's body as nearly parallel to the long side of the *manège* as possible. The outside legs pass and cross over the inside ones.

The rider's weight is on the inside seat bone; the inside hand is opened a little, the thumb pointing in the direction of the movement. The outside rein supports by being on the neck. The outside leg is laid flat on the horse behind the girth to push the horse both forwards and sideways, whilst the inside one is acting on the girth.

All these movements are best commenced in walk before being attempted in trot.

A/B/C:
Three phases of the half-turn on the quarters.

Half turn on the quarters – demi-pirouette

This difficult movement should not be attempted until the horse has acquired an acceptable carriage and is capable, as a result, of lightening his forehand and carrying the weight over the quarters.

A.

B.

The purpose of the turn is: C.

(1) To eradicate still further the resistance to be found in the
    quarters by increasing our control over them. In this
    instance they have to be held in place to prevent the horse
    turning on his centre.
(2) To supple the shoulders in the same way that the forehand
    turn suppled the quarters.
(3) To re-balance the horse by lightening the forehand. The
    forehand turn lightened the quarters in similar fashion
    and both therefore contribute to the overall balance.

From an established walk the turn is preceded by a half-halt.
If we wish to make the turn from left to right, the right rein is
opened to lead the horse round; the left rein supports and is laid
against the neck preventing too much movement forward and
limiting the bend of the neck. Both hands are carried to the right.
    The left leg, held flat behind the girth (position B) prevents the
quarters slipping away to that side whilst the right leg controls
the turn and, with a little help from its neighbour, maintains the
impulsion. By far the most powerful incentive, however, is for
the rider to place the weight on the outside seat bone so as to
push the horse over in the required direction.

Ideally, the forefeet and the outside hindfoot will move on the pivot of the inside hindleg.

(A useful way of obtaining the turn is from a half-*volte*, just as the forehand turn can be obtained from the reverse half-*volte*. The half-volte is progressively decreased in size until it becomes a turn on the quarters and does so without endangering the forward impulse.)

Rein-back

This much misunderstood movement should be left alone until the horse is more advanced in his training. Nothing is less edifying than seeing a horse, or a pony ridden by a largely untutored child, hauled backwards by brute force.

The horse can be prepared for the movement in the stable and in-hand but before attempting it under saddle the square halt has to be established and the suppleness and flexibility of the joints increased.

The easy way is to bring the horse to halt square and on the bit with poll and lower jaw flexed and relaxed – that is a prerequisite of the movement. The legs are put on in the aid asking the horse to step forward in walk (on the impulsion button or, in practice, just a shade behind) and as the horse begins his

The rein-back in correct two-time. The rider has over-emphasised the lightening of the seat in this instance.

Oh dear! The rein-back as it should not be done.

response the hands close on the reins (in the third effect, the direct rein of opposition). To ensure that the hands do not move *back* to *pull*, the elbows should be closed into the sides. The voice, which the horse understands, can also be used and it is helpful if the seat is lightened by a slight forward inclination of the trunk. Momentarily the leg aid is reduced and when the horse obeys the block effect of the hands by going back we can release the driving pressure of the legs whilst keeping them lightly in place.

After two or three steps at the most, the legs are applied again and the hands open to permit the horse to move off in walk. It is an exercise which horses find difficult and there is never any need to ask for five or six steps even when the horse is adept at moving back in a straight line.

If the rein-back is overdone or forced the horse stiffens in the back, even hollowing it, and moves his quarters sideways.

Should the horse not at first understand that he is to move backwards, ride forward and then start again. If necessary, have an assistant tap his front lightly, to emphasise still further what is wanted of him.

(It is possible, and is often advocated, to apply the reins alternately, but whilst effective it can be a little more difficult for the rider. If it is not done with some sensitivity the horse, too, may become a little alarmed and resist the aids.)

Section 4

Chapter 8

Jumping

The work on the flat provides the foundation for the jumping exercises. Properly executed, the school movements prepare the horse in the best possible way. The work develops, supples and balances the horse; it ensures a willing obedience and submission and it increases the rider's control. All these factors contribute materially to the horse's gymnastic ability and, therefore, to his subsequent performance over fences.

So long as they are not overjumped or overfaced, the majority of horses enjoy jumping and seem to regard it as relaxation after

(Above):
Jumping forms a part of the horse's lunge lessons, but loose jumping is even more beneficial. It teaches the horse to judge a fence on his own account and is a great confidence-builder.

Loose schooling can be used as an extension of the lunge work. It encourages initiative in the horse and increases his confidence.

The rider in the jumping position with the horse, the stallion Winston, admirably framed between hand and leg.

the frequently demanding school work. There are the occasional horses who are not entirely enthusiastic about jumping but ones that steadfastly refuse to leave the ground are rare. Almost any horse can be taught by progressive exercises to jump fences up to 1.2m (4ft) in height and/or width.

Jumping the horse on the lunge is a useful introduction to jumping and it allows the horse to adjust his balance and stride without the distraction of the rider's weight (and sometimes of the hands). After a very few lessons the horse should operate freely and with confidence over an upright fence of about 90cm (3ft) and over a parallel of the same height and with a 1.2m (4ft) spread.

It is not necessary initially to make the latter a true parallel; it is easier for the horse if the second element is placed 15cm (6in) higher than the first to give something of a staircase effect. In both cases the provision of a ground-line and a distance pole will help the horse to acquire jumping technique and develop a degree of self-initiative. The distance pole needs to be placed 3m (10ft) in front of the fence and it not only assists the horse to judge the approach and take-off but will also prevent any tendency to rush.

The fences should be jumped out of trot and on both the left and right reins. On landing the horse may make a few strides at canter, which is of no consequence, but he must then be asked to return to trot and then to walk before he jumps another fence.

Jumping on the lunge has every possible advantage but it can produce a problem unless the trainer is adept in the use of the rein and appreciates how easily inexpert or unthinking use of the lunge in these circumstances can encourage a most un-desirable habit – that of jumping to the left or right.

The horse must jump the fence from a straight approach and continue for a few strides after landing on the same line. He must not be jumped on the arc of a circle with his head and body inclined towards the trainer's hand by the rein, otherwise he is being taught to jump to one side or the other. (Later in the ridden training we can jump on a circle to improve accuracy and balance, but to do so on the lunge is usually counter-produc-tive.) For that reason the trainer has to move parallel to the horse, not asking him to return to the circle until a few strides after landing.

Phases of the jump

A particular benefit to be derived from lungeing over fences is the opportunity it affords the rider to study the attitude of the horse in the phases of the jump. These are regarded as being

A balanced approach to the fence with the rider's seat in light contact.

Immediately before take-off with the rider in perfect balance.

An exemplary bascule *in the flight phase.*

The rider straightens the trunk in the landing preparatory to the get-away stride

take-off, flight and landing, with the possible addition at either end of the spectrum of the approach and getaway strides.

The ideal which should be imprinted on the rider's mind is that *if a position is maintained in which the rider sits in balance with the horse and, therefore, without interference with the movement, the outline in each of the phases should not differ from that assumed when the horse is jumping free.*

An analysis of the phases shows the horse raising the head in the *approach*, in order to focus on the fence and judge the take-off, and bringing the hindlegs under the body preparatory to entering the next phase.

At the point of *take-off* the hindlegs are brought further under the body whilst the forelegs lift upwards the forepart of the body, an action necessarily accompanied by the raising of the head and neck. Finally, the engaged quarters thrust powerfully upwards, propelling the horse into the *flight* phase, when head and neck are extended and the forelegs tucked up. Almost simultaneously the horse forms an arc over the fence with the back rounded and head and neck at full stretch. (The word used to describe this attitude is the French, *bascule*.)

On *landing* the forelegs are outstretched and the feet meet the ground *one after another*. For a split second, therefore, the horse's weight is carried on one foot. In order to adjust the balance, re-distributing the weight carried over the forehand, the head and neck, acting as the balancing agents for the body mass, are raised. When the hindlegs touch down the head and neck are lowered and the horse goes into the *getaway* stride.

Should the rider hinder or unbalance the horse, either by the disposition of the bodyweight or the limiting action of the hand, at any point during the leap the outline will be altered, the jump made less effective and the horse will be subjected to additional and unnecessary strain.

Mounted jumping

The first ridden exercises begin with the pole grid which has to be ridden from both directions. The poles, three at first and then five of them, are placed between 1.2m(4ft) and 1.8m(6ft) apart depending on the stride of the horse and one needs to take particular care to get the distance right.

With a shortened stirrup the horse is ridden in a few circles to either hand in rising trot. When the horse is moving actively with a regular rhythm, dropping the nose and relaxing the jaw on either side of his mouth a wide turn is ridden from which a straight approach can be made to the grid.

Still in rising trot, the legs act in time with the stride to make the horse cross the grid without alteration to the speed and

The young horse Dr Dolittle (Paddy) trotting a single pole as an introduction to the grid exercises.

Paddy crossing a three-pole grid freely enough but without any significant stretching.

Much improved activity and a lowering of head and neck, the back becoming rounded.

rhythm but, of course, with increased flexion of the joints.

Contact has to be maintained with the mouth by relaxed elbows and hands moving forward to follow and allow the stretching movement of the head and neck. It is just as important to ride accurately and correctly in the jumping exercises as in those on the flat. *Once the rider becomes careless in respect of either rhythm, contact or balance the quality of the work deteriorates and will be reflected in the horse's performance.*

The usual failings in the simple grid exercise, other than losing the rhythm, are (a) for the rider to lose contact by letting the rein slip through the fingers, and (b) for the trunk to be inclined too far forward, that is in advance of the movement and thus out of balance with the horse. In fact, a great many of the refusals experienced by novice riders are caused, as it were, by the rider jumping the fence before they have got there.

The first jump can be made by moving the last pole 3m (10ft) (double the trotting distance) from the penultimate one and raising it to make a small fence between 45cm and 50cm (18–20in). The rider needs hardly alter the position over this fence, it is, after all, only a very small obstacle, but hands and shoulders need to be advanced a little in order to follow the extension of the neck. The legs remain active in time with the stride through the grid, being applied more firmly in the final squeeze as the horse passes the penultimate pole.

Simple combinations

When 'jump perfect' over this small fence the exercise can be made more demanding by the addition of a second fence at the same height built 5.4m (18ft) from the first. This distance allows the horse one *non-jumping canter* stride between the two fences, that is between landing over the first and the take-off point for the second. (The average canter stride for a horse is between 3.3m and 3.6m (11–12ft) and becomes longer as the speed increases. In general, the optimum take-off point for a 1.2m (4ft) fence is one and a third times the height. At this height and when the approach is from trot 5.4m (18ft) is an easily manageable distance for anything except a very big, long-striding horse.)

To ride this simple combination the rider crosses the grid in trot as before. As the horse *lands* over the first element of the combination the legs are put on firmly; almost inevitably the horse will take one canter stride and the leg action is then repeated even more decisively to ask for the take-off over the second element. Let the horse go on for a few strides in canter before bringing him back to circle quietly at trot and then at walk before asking for another jump. (Always in schooling, bring the horse back to a slower pace after a jump, but equally make sure

Jumping exercises

Excellent engagement of the hindlegs accompanied by lowering and stretching of head and neck and full use of the rounded back.

Crossing poles set on the circle with the bend maintained. The engagement of the limbs and the use made of a rounded back is noteworthy.

This picture demonstrates the value of the poles as a strengthening exercise leading, particularly, to full flexion of the hindleg joints.

Using the distance pole to help the horse over the first small, cross-pole fence.

The distance pole moved in to provide an exercise in agility. A good lead-in to the 'bounce' fence which comes later in the training progression.

A small spread fence encourages the horse to develop scope – the ability to stretch out over parallels.

The Vee-fence exercise on a circle teaches the horse to operate accurately over the fence. On landing he will turn to the right to jump the fence in the background.

Two plain uprights jumped off the circle.

Paddy dealing with a small bounce double preceded by a distance pole.

Winston in a one-stride double.

A useful exercise in which the second element allows for three options.

Winston jumping the first element.

The more difficult A-Frame fence.

A/B/C:
Poles laid on the ground ensure straightness throughout the jumping exercise.

A.

B.

(Opposite Above): C

(Opposite Below):
The horse is halted in front of the fence so as to instil obedience and check any tendency to rush.

that he is allowed to canter on for a few strides after landing so that there is no encouragement for him to 'dwell' in the getaway stride. One must *ride* away from the fence.)

The words 'firm' and 'decisive' in relation to the leg action are deliberate. They mean just that, and the leg aid must never be allowed to deteriorate into a vulgar kick which disturbs the rider's balance and in consequence that of the horse. It is just as important to observe the measure of the aids when jumping or riding cross-country as when schooling on the flat. They will, of necessity, be stronger, but it is pointless to teach the horse obedience to the lightest of aids on the flat and then to employ extra strong and disturbing leg actions when jumping. It is also unnecessary. Indeed, by using over-strong aids in the schooling over fences we are reducing the range of pressures at our disposal and are coming close to *punishing* the horse into the fence instead of *riding* him. If you kick to jump a 60cm (2ft) fence what is there left to do when the horse is asked to make a special effort over a big and difficult obstacle?

The next step is to raise the fences to 60cm (2ft) using whatever materials are available to make the jump look solid. The increase in height is insignificant but it involves the rider closing the angle between upper body and thigh still more whilst concentrating on getting the weight down through the knees to the ankle. The closing of the body/thigh angle causes the seat to be raised a little from the saddle at take-off. The shoulders have then to be taken further forward with the elbow and hand advancing to follow the mouth. The seat needs to return lightly to the saddle on landing – an important point for it contributes to the rider's security in the event of the horse pecking.

Finally, make the last element of the double a parallel 60cm (2ft) high and 1.2m (4ft) in width. This will cause both rider and horse to be more active in the approach and take-off. Initially, so as to improve the horse's judgement of this new obstacle, fix the second element of the parallel some 7.5cm (3in) higher than the first.

These exercises involving the jumping of small fences from a grid approach are valuable because they encourage balanced jumping in a state of calm. Additionally, they increase the suppleness and gymnastic ability and give the horse confidence in himself. They ensure, of course, that the horse will arrive automatically at the right point of take-off and that in itself improves his judgement of the fence.

The last exercise can be extended by following a three-pole trotting grid with a 60cm (2ft) fence 3m (10ft) away. Then allow 5.4m (18ft) (one non-jumping stride) before putting up a parallel 10m (33ft) away (two non-jumping strides) measuring 75cm

(2.5 ft) in height and 1.2m (4ft) in width.

This calls for concentration by both partners in the enterprise and the rider needs to be quite clear about when the legs are to be put on. The one-stride distance calls for the legs to be applied twice – once on landing over the first element and once more to ask for the take-off over the second. Two strides between the fences require the legs to act with increasing definition *three* times, the last decisive squeeze, not kick, asking for take-off.

For the rider to concentrate on good style in jumping is not a pious declaration of intent. Good style, on the contrary, is highly practical since any deviation from the ideal disturbs the balance of the horse and probably his confidence too.

The principal faults, which occur even in experienced riders, are:

(1) *Rounding the shoulders and dropping the head.* It loosens and unbalances the seat. The back should be flat and be carried as nearly as possible in line with the horse's spine in the take-off and flight phases of the jump.
(2) *Lowering the toe and raising the heel upwards.* It obviates the effective use of the lower leg. It pitches the rider forward to the detriment of balance and security. It displaces knee and thigh, causing the weight to be carried in advance of the movement, and makes it very easy for the rider to exit over the shoulder should the horse peck on landing.
(3) *Kicking with the heels.* A failing already discussed.

The jumping seat

The seat is no more than a modification of the balanced position adopted for flatwork and is based on a shortened stirrup leather. The seat is then pushed further to the back of the saddle and when the rider stands in the stirrup irons the seat will be raised a little above it.

The effect of the shorter leather is to make the angle at the knee, between thigh and lower leg, more acute and to close correspondingly the angle between upper body and thigh when the shoulders are inclined forward in front of the hips.

The seat allows the rider to assume a more forward position to correspond with the horse's advanced centre of balance when jumping and it places the weight, via the bent knee, more upon the ball of the foot and less upon the seat bones.

The salient features of the seat are as follows:

(1) Trunk inclines forward from the hips.
(2) Head held up, rider looks directly to the front.

(3) Back held flat with shoulders open.

(4) Elbows lightly into the side. Using a necessarily shorter rein the hands are held either side of the withers and a little below them, but not so low as to break the straight line from elbow to bit.

(5) Seat in light contact with saddle or minimally raised from it.

(6) Knee pointed and well down the saddle so that the thigh is in contact.

(7) Lower leg held slightly to rear of the girth and in contact, toe raised and weight sunk into the heel.

Distance poles

So far the horse has been helped by the correct siting of the grid and the combination of small fences to arrive correctly at his point of take-off. But there is a point when we should remove that dependence and encourage the horse to work out the problems for himself – with, of course, help from the rider and some carefully planned fences. However, it is still advisable to retain a distance pole in front to prevent rushing and to provide some assistance in the judging of the take-off. (So far as the rider is concerned the distance pole is a useful aid in 'seeing the stride'.)

Two fences can be built, one each side of the schooling area. The height by degrees can be raised to 90cm (3ft) but both must be solid in appearance and both should be supplied with a ground-line. One can be a straightforward upright and the other a parallel. Build the latter with a 1.2m (4ft) spread and have the second element a hole higher than the first, and approach from trot. To encourage the horse provide wings to the fences. In the absence of properly constructed wings a pole resting on the standard at one end and on a bale or something similar at the other will serve the purpose. Once the horse is within the enclosing wings, which at the standard end will be considerably higher than the obstacle, it is easier for him to jump the fence than to attempt to run out to one side or the other. We should not, however, place too much reliance on the wings, nor allow the horse to do so. By gradual stages as the horse becomes increasingly confident we should aim to dispose of them altogether.

The distance poles can then be varied so as to give one or two non-jumping strides, and finally the fences can be approached from canter with the distance pole placed 13.5m (44ft) away to give three non-jumping strides between landing over the pole and take-off over the fence.

Changes of direction

Jumping single fences is relatively undemanding. Jumping which calls for precisely executed changes of direction is considerably more complex and puts a premium on the approach and the maintenance of impulsion and balance. The figure-of-eight is the ideal exercise in these respects.

The exercise involves four fences sited on a figure-of-eight which can be made as large as the schooling area allows.

The fences can be varied but should initially be kept very low, certainly no bigger than 75–90cm (2.5ft–3ft) and should be preceded by a one-stride distance pole set at 5.4m (18ft) from the fence, which will be approached from trot. In effect this involves trotting round the 'short' sides at the top and bottom of the figure-of-eight.

Follow this by placing the poles to give two non-jumping strides, or three if space is available. After which dispense with the distance poles in front of the second and fourth fence, siting those fences so as to vary the number of non-jumping strides between one and two, and three and four.

The exercise is, amongst other things, a lead-in to the change of direction and leg at canter which, ultimately, may have to be made in mid-air over a fence.

(Before attempting the figure-of-eight exercise over fences put out some strategically spaced markers and ride the figure very accurately at trot, keeping to the track exactly without cutting corners and whilst maintaining the impulsion and rhythm.)

The angled fence

To get closer to the ideal of changing direction over the fence begin by placing a small fence at the centre of the figure-of-eight. Trot the figure, jumping the fence at an angle until the horse can perform the exercise with complete accuracy, then go on to jumping from canter, returning to trot round the short ends and then striking off on the opposite canter lead as the approach is made off the opposite diagonal.

Thereafter increase the height to 75cm (2.5ft). The fence, though not large, adds a complication to the exercise. Sited as it is and approached from an angle it invites the unsteady horse to run out and down the line of the fence. Approaching from the left the horse can run out to the right and along the obstacle and vice versa. It demands, therefore, concentration on the part of the rider and obedience and some initiative from the horse.

The extension to the exercise and the introduction to the change in mid-air is accomplished by placing a fence of crossed poles in the centre of the arena but parallel to the long sides. The crossed poles encourage the horse (and the rider) to jump accu-

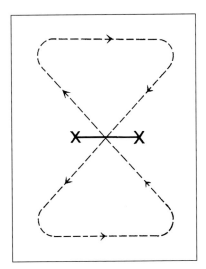

An exercise to teach both horse and rider to jump at an angle to the fence. A low pole is quite sufficient as a beginning.

One practical application of the angle-jumping exercise is to counter a run-out by the horse. In this instance the horse has run-out to the left and the error is corrected by jumping at an angle to the right of the fence.

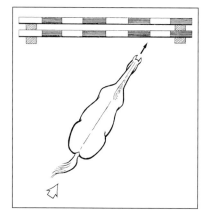

An exercise in making changes of direction.

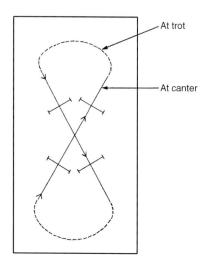

At trot

At canter

rately over the centre, and to do that the circles have to be ridden with equal accuracy if the approach is to allow them to do so.

A single circle ridden at trot commences the exercise. As the horse jumps the fence, the rider has to incline the horse's head and the upper part of their own body in the direction of the movement whilst applying the canter leg aids. In almost every instance the horse will land in canter and on the correct lead. The exercise has to be practised on both reins and when the strike-offs are established the circle can be ridden in both directions at canter. Thereafter the full figure-of-eight can be ridden.

Bounce fence and jumping grid

Bounce fences (those allowing no stride between the two elements) increase the gymnastic ability and suppleness of the horse and can also, along with the jumping grid, be looked upon as a strengthening exercise.

As an introduction put up two small fences 3.6m (12ft) apart with a distance pole 5.4m (18ft) from the combination. Trot into the fence strongly. Apply the legs on landing and, since there is no room for the horse to take a stride, he will 'bounce' out over the second element. A more advanced exercise is to include a bounce fence as part of a combination of related fences. For instance, one might commence with an upright, followed 10m (33ft) away (two non-jumping strides) by the bounce combination and then by an obstacle placed so as to give either one or two non-jumping strides. The distances can of course, be varied to produce progressively more difficult exercises.

A useful, easily constructed training aid, usually much enjoyed by horses and their riders, is the jumping grid. It is a line of up to six fixed fences, 45cm (18ins) high and placed 3.6m (12ft) apart, which is ridden at canter. If the side can be enclosed by a rail so much the better.

Fence variety

Essentially all fences fall into one of four categories, although, of course, the appearance can be varied by the addition of filling materials etc. and the substitution of walls, gates, planks, etc. for the basic pole. There are *upright, staircase, parallel* and *pyramid* fences, all of which should be included in the horse's training since they present different problems in respect of take-offs and angle of descent.

At an *upright* the take-off zone, in general terms, is between a distance equal to the height of the fence and up to one and one-third times its height – the latter being closer to optimum take-off point than otherwise.

For the fence to be jumped successfully the point of take-off and landing should be equidistant from the bottom of the fence. The horse reaches the highest point of the arc made when jumping the fence when he is directly over the top of the obstacle.

The upright fence is the most difficult to jump since if the horse takes off too close he hits the fence on the way up, whereas if he stands off too far he is likely to hit the fence with his hindlegs in the descent.

A ground pole, judiciously placed, reduces the difficulty and can be used to teach the horse how to judge his take-off. Placed in front of the fence at the appropriate distance in relation to its height it can be used to produce a correct take-off since the horse judges the latter for the most part by looking at the bottom of the fence. A further pole on the ground at a similar distance on the landing side will control the angle of descent if it should become too steep, as the horse will reach out to clear it.

A *staircase* is a much easier and more encouraging obstacle. It is a fence built with two or three bars set at ascending heights, as in the case of a triple bar obstacle, and its shape corresponds to the parabola of the leap. The highest point of the leap will be in line with the highest element in the fence and it occurs in the middle of the flight phase. The landing is well out from the fence and the angle of descent less steep than over an upright. In consequence the getaway stride after landing is relatively long in comparison with the shorter stride following an upright.

A simple practice course.

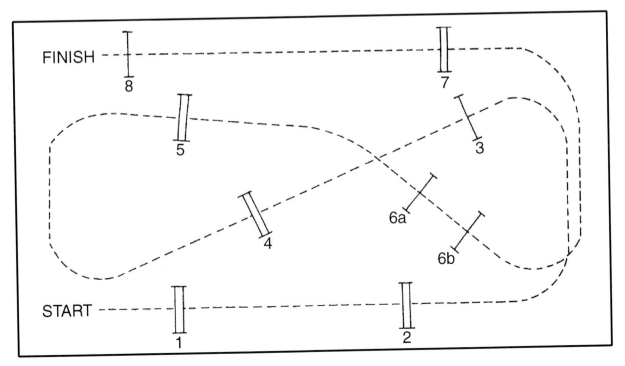

These are factors which have to be taken into account when estimating distances between combination fences.

Parallel fences comprise two elements which in a 'true' parallel are of the same height. Lowering the first element introduces a staircase quality and makes the fence easier to jump.

It might seem that a horse has to take off well away from a fence of this nature and he may, indeed, do so, but it involves his making a very big jump with increased effort and a probable decrease in accuracy.

The most successful way to jump a parallel is to take off closer to the fence than would be advisable in the case of an upright. The reason is because the horse has to reach the highest point of the leap when he is closer to the rear bar than to the one in front of the fence. In consequence the landing is well out from the fence and as a result of the less abrupt angle of descent the getaway stride is longer.

A *pyramid* fence comprises three elements, the first and last of equal height and the central one higher. It can be jumped from both directions but it must not be built too big or with too great a spread as the horse cannot see the final element. It comes, however, within the category encompassing spread fences and the getaway stride is longer than with an upright.

Distances

With combinations of fences 1.2m (4ft) in height and with spreads of the same measurement, the following distances take into account differences in the angle of descent and their effect on the length of the getaway stride. They are based on an average canter stride of 3.3–3.6m (11–12ft).

Upright to upright	7.2m (24ft)	one non-jumping stride
	10–10.5m (33–35ft)	two non-jumping strides
Upright to spread	6.9m (23ft)	one non-jumping stride
	9.6–10.2m (32–33ft)	two non-jumping strides
Spread to upright	7.5m (25ft)	one non-jumping stride
	10.5–11.1m (35–36ft)	two non-jumping strides
Spread to spread	7.2m (24ft)	one non-jumping stride
	10–10.5m (33–35ft)	two non-jumping strides

(The same formula is applied to three non-jumping strides 13.5m (44ft); four 16.8m (55ft) and five 20.1m (66ft), the addition or subtraction of a foot between types of fences being the same. Fences are *related* between 11.9m and 24m (39ft and 79ft) apart. Below 11.7m (38ft) they become combinations.)

Chapter 9
Cross-country Riding

There is a more rumbustious, freer character involved with riding across country over obstacles and natural hazards, and both horse and rider have to adapt their technique accordingly. Indeed, it is not untrue to say that much of the school work and jumping exercises carried out within the training areas are no more than a preparation for riding outside the constrictions imposed by 'walls' and 'long' and 'short' sides. For that reason much emphasis should be given to hacking out over varied terrain demanding continual adjustments of balance.

The essence of early cross-country training is concerned with the need to:

(1) Accustom the horse to cope with natural terrain, including going up and down hills in balance and maintaining an easy rhythm.
(2) Jump a variety of low, fixed obstacles and natural hazards, including water, out of his stride and both up and down hill.

Fences, since they are fixed, should be small and inviting and one has also to seek natural obstacles like ditches and streams.

The rider's position

Across country the rider adopts the jumping position, placing the weight over the centre of balance and keeping the legs in contact. The faults to be avoided are straightening the leg so that the contact and flexion of knee and ankle are lost and the seat is taken too far out of the saddle. Just as common a failing is for the rider to disturb the balance by getting in front of the movement.

The pace to adopt in cross-country riding is a good swinging canter and once the horse has settled into the rhythm (and all horses develop their own comfortable cruising speed) the rider's concern is to remain in balance whilst keeping steady contact with hands and legs.

However, there is a noticeable difference between horses ridden in the schooling area and being ridden in the great outdoors. Horses that in the school take up a nice light contact and may need active legs to maintain impulsion can be quite different in the open. The natural impulsion is increased and the formerly light-mouthed character may take a stronger hold of his bridle.

This is natural and to be encouraged, but clearly it has to be kept within reasonable bounds, but without the rider fighting the horse to keep control. Fighting against a strong, pulling horse does no good at all. The horse's excitement increases; he pulls even harder against the discomfort caused by the bit and he becomes less and less receptive to his rider. For the rider, too, it is an unnecessarily exhausting business.

There is a knack in restraining a pulling horse which is acquired with experience and it has nothing to do with brute force. The first rule is to keep calm, thereafter restraint can be imposed by straightening the upper body so that the weight, in fact, is somewhat behind the centre of gravity and the seat a little out of the saddle to allow the powerful back muscles to be used to full advantage.

The lower leg, too, may advance just a little. The hands act by one of them holding a steady contact whilst the other closes and opens in firm squeezes. One should not, however, always check with the same hand. The horse gets used to it and he stiffens that side of his mouth in resistance because we have more or less provided him with a base against which to pull, even though the check is followed by a release of pressure. Constant pressure from one or both hands is even worse and is, indeed, an encouragement to the horse to pull even more strongly.

The effective way to use the hands in conjunction with the restraining aids of the body is to make the checks with alternate hands so that the base against which the horse can resist is continually switched from one side of the mouth to the other. When the horse responds and comes back to his 'natural' canter speed the rider can resume his position poised over the centre of balance and revert to the policy of minimal intervention.

Up and down

Riding across country must inevitably involve traversing slopes and hills. Riding uphill the horse has to be able to employ the full propulsive power of his quarters and so the rider needs to fold the upper body forward from the hips so as to give the quarters complete freedom. The hands must allow any extension of the neck that is made whilst keeping a light contact with the mouth.

Going downhill is not so easy and the young horse needs to be introduced gradually to slopes of increasing severity. Downhill slopes should be ridden first at walk with the rider's legs insisting that the horse moves forward steadily and *straight*.

If the quarters are allowed to swing out so that the horse is across the slope there is a real danger of his legs slipping from under him. If the horse attempts to hurry he can be restrained by the fingers closing on the rein. The contact with the hand is, however, necessary to the horse since it allows him to relate his balance to what is a still point.

Whilst the upper body should most certainly not be allowed to overweight the forehand by being inclined too far to the front, it should just as certainly not be inclined to the rear with the legs poked out in front. The horse does need to have his hindlegs well underneath him and for that reason sitting well back over the quarters is to be discouraged. Conversely, if the trunk is inclined too far forward the transference of weight to the front end may force the horse into going faster and faster in order to keep a semblance of balance. As in all things moderation is to be encouraged.

Position

In fact, moderation combined with reasonable prudence is the secret of cross-country riding, together with an ability to adapt to the circumstances.

In general, it is advisable for the rider to adopt a less than absolute forward position over cross-country fences. It would, for instance, be unwise to get in front of the centre of gravity at a drop fence. It is far better and much more secure to hold the body in the vertical plane and 'slip' the reins.

The more experience that the young horse can obtain over a variety of small cross-country obstacles, including drops, banks and small step-type obstacles, the better will be his balance. Furthermore, he will gain confidence in himself and his rider.

A very good training exercise, if the facilities are available, is to build a number of small obstacles, even if they are no more than stout logs or low piles of brush on tracks through a small piece of woodland and to ride over them at a steady canter letting the horse jump out of his stride.

Refusals

Before concluding this chapter we should consider the matter of the horse refusing at a fence. In a carefully planned and executed training programme refusals should either not occur or occur only rarely. It is, nonetheless, appropriate to remind ourselves of why and how horses decline to jump.

Horses refuse for one or other of the following reasons:

(1) They are over-faced, either by the fence being too high or because they lack the experience to tackle it successfully.

(2) They may be sore from having jarred their legs or from a strained back.

(3) They stop if they believe the act of jumping will cause them pain. Ill-fitting saddles which pinch as the back is arched over a fence are a sure way to cause refusals. So, of course, is a rider whose incompetence causes him to jab the horse in the mouth at take-off. Horses that have been compelled to jump when their muscles ached or their shins were sore may refuse long after the trouble has cleared up. A bad experience at a fence resulting in loss of confidence may cause problems at similar fences and it will take time and patience to get the horse going happily again.

(4) Rider error, or just plain incompetence, is one of the most common sources leading to refusals. Young horses cannot be taught to jump by inexperienced riders at novice level.

A principal failing in the less than expert is the obsession with not being left behind. In many ways it is commendable but it can be carried too far and with disastrous results.

If the rider lifts the seat out of the saddle in the approach, inclining the trunk well forward, it is very likely that contact with the mouth will be lost. The weight of the rider throws the horse on his forehand and despite those flailing legs and increased speed the position worsens as the horse gets into the take-off zone. The easiest and probably the most sensible thing for the horse to do in those circumstances is to stop – and he usually does. Speed, incidentally, only causes a horse to flatten the trajectory of the leap. The ideal jump is made from impulsion out of a state of balance.

(5) Horses will refuse when they find themselves wrong at a fence. By doing so they display their good sense and should not be punished for that.

Horses refuse by stopping or by running out. In other words they cease to obey the legs and they cease to go forwards.

All training is, or should be, directed towards obtaining obedience and instant response to the driving aids of the legs but even so, for one reason or another, most of them connected with a faulty or too casual approach, there will be an occasional stop.

If it is a run-out, circle quietly but swiftly in the opposite direction, turn him off the circle and present him at the fence at a slight angle from the side to which he ran out. That is, if he went out to the left bring him in from the left, which makes it nearly impossible for him to run out to the same side again. Be careful, however, not to make the angle too shallow otherwise you are inviting him to run out across the front of the fence.

In training, whether the horse stops dead or runs out, have the fence *lowered* and jump it for two or three days at the lower height before putting it up again – always, of course, assuming that it was not impossibly high to start with.

Chapter 8 mentions how it is possible to cause a horse jumping on the lunge to jump to one side or another by the lunge line not allowing him sufficient freedom to go straight forwards after landing. This is the source of much crooked jumping but it can also develop later in the training. Obviously, the habit creates problems over a course, particularly in the negotiation of short combination fences.

It can be countered and cured by using a 'straightening' pole placed from the top of the upright to the landing side on that side of the fence which the horse favours. First place the pole at right angles to the fence, moving it inwards as the horse becomes accustomed to its presence and jumps the fence freely with the pole in position. When the horse jumps straight with the pole at an angle of, say, 30° to the fence one can consider the habit to have been corrected. The 'A' fence, illustrated, is also an excellent exercise in teaching accurate, precision jumping.

In cross-country jumping the horse has to be allowed to use his own initiative more so than over show fences. Very often the rider will need to encourage the horse at a difficult obstacle but there will be many occasions when we can do nothing but leave it to the horse, sitting as still as we can and 'throwing' the reins at him. If the relationship between horse and rider is right the good horse will then return the compliment and get his rider out of trouble.

A double of logs present no difficulties to the stallion, Picasso.

(Left and Below):
Uphill and downhill fences are essential
obstacles.

A well-built Coffin obstacle is a test of boldness and agility.

The ability to jump water is essential to the cross-country horse.

Over the corner of the Vee rails.

The easier bounce route through the rails.

(Above):
Banks are a feature of almost every cross-country course.

(Right):
A log forms an uphill approach with a drop on the landing side.

(Following two Pages):
A simple rail over a ditch may cause more problems than might be expected.

Straightforward log pile.

Section 5

Chapter 10

The Importance of Conformation

Nothing, except perhaps the British weather, provides so fruitful a topic of conversation in horsy circles as the conformation of the horse. Conformation may be defined as being relative to the skeletal frame and its accompanying muscle formations, to the perfection of the component parts and their symmetrical proportion to each other. The *Oxford English Dictionary* is even more succinct: 'Form depending upon arrangement of parts; structure.'

When purchasing a horse, its conformation, in relation to the purpose required of it, is of supreme importance. (It would, for instance, be foolish to buy a harness horse if one's ambition were to compete in the sport of eventing, and vice versa.)

To the horsemen of the European mainland, the 'beauty classes' of the British show ring may seem to be a quaint irrelevance in comparison with their own performance-tested systems. Classes are adjudicated by one or more often two, very experienced, independent and unpaid judges (qualified, indeed, by experience) who are charged with assessing the merits of the animals brought before them. They are not appraised of the pedigree/performance records etc. of the exhibits and their forbears and so the major consideration in their deliberations is the perfection or otherwise of individual conformation.

It may seem to be a delightfully amateur and, perhaps, peculiarly British way of going on, but it is not without its merits. Certainly the best show-ring judges are among the best in the world when it comes to having an 'eye for a horse' and for the novice their precepts and their example are well-worth following.

(In a perfect world, an intending purchaser should most certainly take account of the horse's pedigree and the performance record of sire, dam and related animals. However, such documentation is not always readily available and one has to rely upon a visual assessment based, one hopes, on experience and an acquired knowledge of the characteristics of the well-made horse and their relevance to the purpose required of it.)

A well-proportioned horse will be naturally balanced with movement which reflects the excellence of the physique. Potentially, therefore, the performance should, all else being equal, exceed that of the horse with conformational deficiencies. Additionally, of course, the correctly formed horse should have a longer working life, for the reason that he is more mechanically efficient than his less well-proportioned brother or sister. It may be more difficult to associate manners with conformation, but without doubt there is a connection between conformation and temperament. It is very possible for a horse to be forced into making resistances because he is asked to perform movements or assume an outline which some failing in his physical make-up makes difficult and which causes discomfort and even pain. If the rider persists and forces the horse to comply, then it is not surprising if the latter becomes soured and resentful. If, for example, the shape and set of the head and neck makes flexion at the poll difficult, and if in that situation a 'head-carriage' is imposed upon the horse by means of some forceful gadget, then we may expect some form of reaction as a result of the pain he experiences.

Breed societies, quite rightly, lay much emphasis on correct conformation, many of them organising judging seminars and training sessions for prospective judges, but for the run-of-the-mill rider/owner there may be little opportunity for constructive study. One suspects indeed, that for many conformation may be regarded as something of an arcane science, surrounded by a phraseology which is similarly obscure.

In fact, the assessment of conformation is not so difficult to master as might be supposed. Furthermore, it is a fascinating exercise and one which might be thought of as being an essential accomplishment for anyone aspiring to successful horse ownership. There are, of course, some fundamental rules to be followed and some knowledge of the basic principles of form and its relationship with intended purpose has to be acquired. Otherwise, an 'eye for a horse' can be developed by practice.

As a start, the diagram of the 'proportional horse' (evolved by Professor Wortley Axe on the basis of the calculations made by French veterinarians, Bourgelat and Duhousset) provides a useful guideline. Indeed, it is well worthwhile taking a tape-measure to a number of horses and comparing the result with Wortley Axe's measurements.

An interesting comparison of the human and equine skeletons.

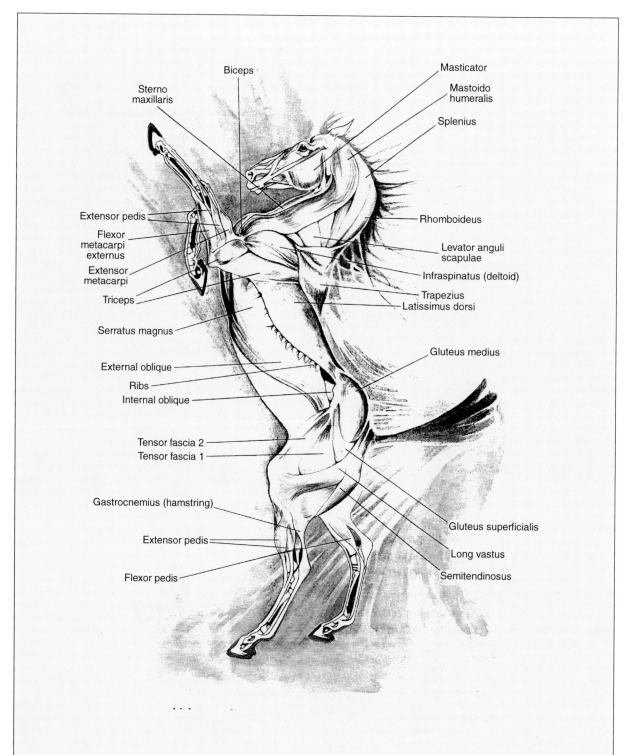

The muscular structure.

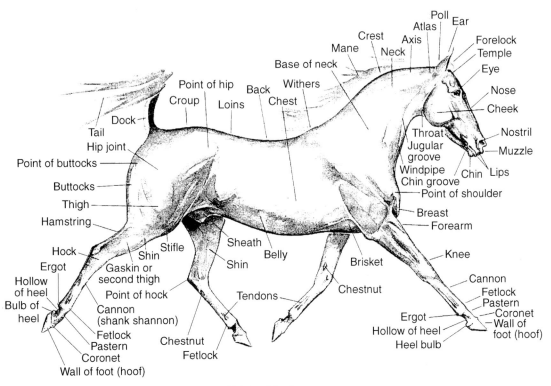

Points of the horse.

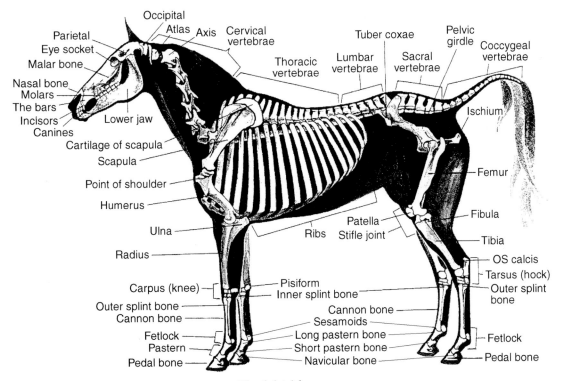

The skeletal frame.

The system of measurements devised by Professor Wortley Axe for assessing the ideally proportioned horse. It is based on two principal units: the length of head and the distance between seat bone and hip.

Length of head = A) point of hock to ground; B) point of hock to fold of stifle; C) chestnut (horny growth on inside of foreleg) to the base of the foot; D) depth of body at girth; E) posterior angle of scapula (shoulder blade), that is at the rear of its juncture with the withers, to the point of the hip; F) fold of stifle to croup.

Seat bone to point of hip = A) seat bone to stifle; B) stifle to point of hip.

Length point of shoulder to seat bone = length of head x 2½.

Height from fetlock to elbow = height from elbow to withers.

Line dropped from seat bone meets point of the hock and continues down the back of the cannon bone.

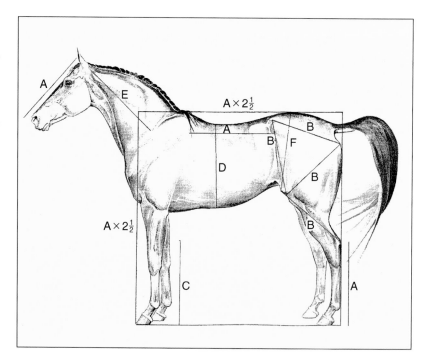

Thereafter, when assessing horses, first stand back and view the whole horse. A good precept is that which tells us that a horse should 'fill the eye'. If there is a noticeable lack of overall symmetry, if one feature seems to predominate over the others or if there is any notable deficiency then whether he fills the eye or not he will not satisfy it.

Conformation does, of course, vary according to the purpose for which the horse is required. At one extreme there is the short, thick proportions and musculature of the heavy draught horse, which are indicative of strength and tractive power but are in no way associated with speed and athletic agility. At the other extreme there is the opposite conformation of the Thoroughbred, based on *length* of proportions and muscles, which is indicative of speed. In between there are horses which incline more or less to one or the other.

Having looked at the horse as a whole, one can then examine the individual components and the relationship to each other in more detail.

The head is as revealing of character and antecedents as anything and can provide a remarkable sum of information about the individual.

Well-bred horses, which one can expect to be alert and responsive with quick reactions, have lean, refined heads, the bone formation being lightly covered with skin. The profile, in all but the Arab, is straight or just slightly concave. In the 'horse of the desert' there is a pronounced 'dish' to the front line of the face which is a much-prized characteristic of the breed and is frequently apparent in the breed's close derivatives.

Horses of more plebeian breeding, often with some cold-blood, heavy horse element in the background, are coarser about the head; the skin covering is thicker and the hair, silky and thin in the well-bred horse, is heavier and wiry. Often there is a tendency towards a convex (Roman nose) profile, a certain sign of cold-blood ancestry often displayed by the big, weight-carrying sorts.

On the whole it is of no great import in an otherwise sound riding horse, unless this not unattractive feature is accompanied by a pronounced bump between eyes which are small and piggy. Such eyes are thought to denote a mean and ungenerous spirit, and they usually do. The bump may or may not be signif-icant, except for its association with an ungenerous eye, but it rarely finds approval with horsemen.

On the other hand a prominent bump between the ears is desirable. This bone represents the occipital crest which is the attachment point for the suspensory ligament of the head and neck – as such it needs to be well-developed if it is to be an effi-cient point of anchorage.

Everyone, one imagines, associates big, expressive eyes as being indicative of a kind, generous nature, but the placement of the eyes is just as critical. In the riding horse, the eyes need to be placed as much to the front of the head as possible and so the forehead must not be too broad. This gives the desirable frontal vision necessary to a horse which is expected to gallop and jump. Heavy horses have the eyes placed to the side of the head, a position which allows for greater lateral vision at the expense of frontal vision. Horses that show the whites of the eye are also to be treated with circumspection, particularly when they also lay back the ears and dilate the nostrils.

Ears are almost as informative as eyes, particularly when viewed from the saddle. They give us warning of the horse's intentions and a good idea of his state of mind at any given moment. I like them to be thinly covered, very mobile and easily pricked. An ear, flicking constantly back and forth, denotes an attentive horse, alert to receive his rider's requests.

Very heavy, overlong ears, covered with a wire-brush of hair and moving sluggishly belong to slow-thinking, phlegmatic characters, tardy in their responses and reactions.

Lop ears are those which are carried out sideways as a result of some loss of nerve control. They are always associated, possibly for no very good reason other than experience, with genuine sorts but their immobility gives no indication of their owner's intentions to the rider.

Nostrils are important since the horse breathes through these air passages. They need to be large and wide to permit maximum inhalation of air when the horse is galloping. Small nostrils are an anathema under any circumstances.

Also of concern is the space between the branches of the jaw. If there is to be sufficient room for the larynx and if the horse is to be able to flex easily at the poll it should be possible to insert one's clenched fist between the jaw bones.

Parrot mouths, where the top jaw overlaps the lower one, or where the opposite is the case and the jaw is under-shot both result in serious bitting problems and make it difficult for the horse to graze normally.

Heads which are out of proportion in relation to the neck are also an unacceptable source of difficulty. The head and neck, which act as a balancing agent for the body, operate to shift the weight forwards or backwards. In general terms the raising of the head and neck (virtually a 40lb blob on the end of a pendulum) transfers the weight from the forehand to the quarters whilst an opposite movement shifts the weight to the forehand. A head that is too big, and, therefore, too heavy for say, a weak, narrow neck will prohibit the desirable shift of the weight over the quarters. A *very* small head, which is less usual, would also act against a proper balance.

A lean head set on a long, graceful neck indicates a speed potential. The opposite, a large head on a shorter, strong neck is a powerful structure often found in heavyweight horses but one which is not associated with great speed. For the most of us the ideal will be somewhere between the two.

An acceptable length of neck in relation to the size of the head is for the length of the former, taken from poll to the highest point of the withers, to be equal to the measurement of the head taken from the poll to the lowest point of the upper lip.

Since the muscles of the neck activate those of the foreleg, causing the latter to be drawn forward, it is absolutely essential that the two sets of muscles are proportionate. In a racehorse, for instance, the forearm will be long, and therefore the neck must be correspondingly so. In a heavy draught horse, where the forearm is short and thick, the shape and musculature of the neck has to be similarly formed.

Two neck formations to be avoided in the riding horse are those termed ewe-neck and swan-neck. In the former the top-line instead of following the graceful curve is concave, the underside of the neck bulging outwards. Remedial schooling will often correct the fault but until that has been accomplished bridling problems are inevitable.

A swan-neck is convex in its upper third and as a result the head is carried in a horizontal plane and thus causes nearly insuperable difficulties with the bitting arrangements. Additionally, this conformation makes a problem for the fitting of the saddle, which is inclined to ride forward so that the girth chafes against the elbow.

The final considerations with the neck are concerned with its juncture to the head at one end and its merging into the shoulder at the other.

Too abrupt a juncture of head and neck, usually found with an excessively thick, short neck which just as usually runs into thick, upright shoulders, results in a thick, fleshy throat that interferes with respiratory freedom.

When the angle of juncture is over-acute the horse is termed 'cock-throttled', a condition in which there is excessive length from the base of the ear to the throat accompanied by a very prominent paratoid gland. As a result the larynx is seriously compressed and the breathing impaired.

At the other end the neck should streamline into the shoulders. But it can only do so if the lower end is sufficiently wide, the neck bones well formed and the *mastoid-humeralis* muscle, at the junction of neck and shoulder, is very well developed. A neck which seems to end before it meets the withers is a serious failing since it is caused by the shoulders being too widely spaced. The shoulder will then be upright and the action inefficient, uneconomical and dreadfully uncomfortable.

Horsemen set great store by a good riding shoulder, 'well laid-back and sloped' – and they are right to do so, since it contributes materially to the effectiveness of the structure in terms of swift, economical movement and the smoothness of the paces. Furthermore, the good shoulder much reduces the effects of concussion in the forelimbs.

The excellence or otherwise of a shoulder depends upon the shape and relative position of three components: withers, scapula (shoulder blade) and humerus, the bone which forms the shoulder joint at the top end and the point of the elbow at the other, where it meets the radius bone of the foreleg. It is necessary to study all three when assessing the fitness of the shoulder for the purpose of riding (or, for that matter, for the purpose of draught when a different set of criteria are applied).

The withers arise from the superior spines of the third to ninth dorsal vertebrae and form the point of attachment for the muscles which not only support the forehand but also govern its movement. The suspensory ligament of the head and neck is attached to the withers as well as the muscles controlling the contraction and extension of the latter. Additionally, the withers provide the attachment point for the muscles of the back, for those activating the ribs in inspiration and for those which attach the scapula to the body. Their formation is, therefore, critical to the performance potential of the horse.

Relatively high, well defined withers provide the most effective attachment for the muscles of the forehand, activating the component parts to the fullest extent. The further back they are placed the more pronounced will be the obliquity of the scapula. Without a clearly defined wither (which is *usually* placed well back) it is not possible for the scapula to be sufficiently sloped to meet the requirements necessary in a good-class riding horse, nor is it made easy for a saddle to be fitted properly and kept in place – a very practical consideration.

With adequate definition of the withers the shoulder blades should be close together at the top. If they are wide apart, as they will be when the withers are flat and loaded with muscles (a condition which is termed 'loaded') the action, instead of being straight and level, tends to become a rolling one. This is of no great consequence in draught breeds in which the blades are frequently quite wide apart and where the criteria are concerned with tractive strength at slow speeds, but it is uneconomical in terms of energy expenditure and performance in the riding horse, as well as being uncomfortable for the rider.

The slope of the scapula is dependent upon the position of the withers, thereafter the concern is with its length, which should be long in relation to the length and position of the humerus, which needs to be short if the leg is to be placed well forward and is to be capable, with the shoulder, of full and free extension. The result of that combination is to produce a long, low stride which covers the ground economically and, of course, contributes to the speed of the movement whilst also being comfortable for the rider.

Where the opposite occurs, that is a short, straight-set scapula arising from flattish withers to join a long humerus, the foreleg is placed much further to the rear. The stride is then shortened significantly and the foreleg displays an up and down movement manifested, necessarily, by high knee action. Such movement obviously limits the length of the stride, causes greater expenditure of effort for less return and increases the concussive effects upon the lower limbs.

Once more this type of conformation and the action which it produces is not detrimental in the draught breeds, so long as it is not unduly exaggerated. A straighter shoulder, for instance, is far more suitable for the fitting of a harness collar than a sloping one, and the shorter stride is more productive for tractive power. Similarly, in the draught horse the withers will be higher than the croup in the interests of effective traction. In the mature riding horse the balance of the body mass is best served when withers and croup are in line or when the former is no more than very slightly higher than the latter. It is natural for the croup to be higher than the withers in growing young-stock, but when a mature horse is lower in front than behind he must inevitably be thrown on the forehand, the ride is made rough and uncomfortable and the forelegs are subjected to strains which may result in unsoundness in the lower limbs. For all that, this type of structure can be conducive to greater speed, witness the greyhound for instance. All in all, however, it is not to be encouraged in the riding horse.

The ideal degrees of inclination in a good riding shoulder are as follows and they can all be easily demonstrated by measurement: *from the junction of the neck with the withers to the point of the shoulder the ideal is 60 degrees; from the highest point of the withers to the point of the shoulder 43 degrees; from the point of the shoulder to the junction of the withers with the back 40 degrees.*

Try measuring half-a-dozen horses with a piece of string, noting the lengths and the degrees of obliquity, and you will soon be able to recognise the good from the bad and the moderate.

One can see the effects of the good shoulder by watching for the length of stride. Surprisingly, perhaps, even when the shoulders are exemplary, the knee is rarely brought in front of the point of the shoulder at walk. At trot it does not reach beyond an imaginary line drawn from the poll to the ground. In gallop the leading foreleg touches the ground in line with the nose and even when the head and neck is fully extended it is rare for the footfall to be in advance of this point.

Behind the withers and the shoulders is the trunk which includes the back up to the point where it joins the quarters. It is supported by the dorsal lumbar vertebrae of the spine, which also carry the weight of the thorax and abdomen.

In assessing the proportions of the trunk there are two inescapable rules of thumb to be observed.

(1) *The depth of the horse through the girth, that is from the top of the withers to the deepest part of the body behind the elbow, should equal the measurement from this last point to the ground.*

(2) *After that the length of the back measured from the rear of the withers to the croup should be short when compared with the measurement from the point of the shoulder to the last of the 'false' ribs. The greater the difference the better and the ideal is probably for the last measurement to be double the length of the first.*

Depth through the girth is important because it allows room for the lungs and for them to be expanded without restriction. Occasionally, depth is related to 'heart room', which is nonsense. There is always sufficient room for the heart, the concern here is with the respiratory ability.

Good depth through the girth gives the appearance of the horse being short-legged. Horses that look to be 'on the leg', or 'show a lot of daylight' between the girth and the ground are only rarely possessed of exceptionally long legs. It is far more likely that they *seem* to have long legs because they are insufficiently deep in the girth.

The ribs also contribute to depth. There are eight 'true' ribs, followed by a further ten 'false' ribs. The 'true' ribs are attached to both vertebrae and sternum bone (thus *sternal* ribs), whereas the 'false' (*asternal*) ribs are attached only to vertebrae.

To be deep through the girth the 'true' ribs need to be long, and in the riding horse they have to be flatter than the 'false' ribs so that the rider's thighs and knees lie flat behind the tricep muscles. 'False' ribs need also to be long rather than otherwise but they have to be nicely rounded, or 'well-sprung'. They lie over the kidneys and other vital organs, so length and an ample rounding are essential factors. If they are short, when they may also be poorly sprung, the animal is pre-disposed to 'running up light' and will be difficult to maintain in condition when he is in work. Such horses take on a shape reminiscent of the conformation of a greyhound in the post-abdominal area leading to the quarters. Almost invariably a problem is caused in the fitting of the saddle since it will continually slip back, particularly in hilly countries.

Finally, there is the condition termed 'short of a rib'. This occurs when the distance between the last rib and the hip bone is more than usually long. The distance between the two should not in perfection come near to exceeding the breadth of a man's hand. When it does there is a notable slackness in the area which has to be accounted as a serious structural fault. Horses that are 'short of a rib' are always difficult to keep in condition when put to hard work. In the case of mares it is permissible for the distance between the two points to be slightly longer than that in the male horse.

Some of the heavy draught breeds, particularly the Clydesdales perhaps, lack depth through the girth because the 'true' ribs are round rather than flat. The Arab, always something of a special case, because of the structural differences which are peculiar to the breed, will very rarely indeed be 'slack' in his middle. This is because of the Arab's *17 ribs, 5 lumbar vertebrae and 16 tail vertebrae which ensures a relatively short back structure and obviates the possibility of being 'short of a rib'. (The Thoroughbred and most other breeds follow the 18–6–18 pattern).* Very often, however, even if it is not entirely desirable, the Arab can be somewhat flat over the withers. There are, of course, Arabs with bad shoulders, but very often, even with a less than well-defined withers, the shoulder is quite adequate in its relation to the overall structure – which goes to show that the breed is just that bit 'different' from others.

Of enormous importance in the riding horse is the back. It has to be able to carry a saddle well (if it does not there is no point in looking further) and it has to be strong enough and of a shape that ensures its ability to take the weight of the rider as well. To do so the muscular development on either side of the spine has to be strong and the back needs to rise slightly to the croup.

Broad backs, in relation to the size of the horse are not, however, desirable. They may be strong but they cause saddle fitting problems and are of no use to the short-legged rider. Furthermore, they are usually associated with flattish withers and an inhibited action.

Departures from the normal are hollow, or 'sway' backs, and the unprepossessing convex or 'roach' back. Hollow backs may occur with age but in young horses they are a serious conformation fault, even if they are held to give a comfortable ride. A roach back is strong but desperately uncomfortable and inhibitive of the action, which is shortened significantly. Roach-backed horses usually 'forge' or 'click', that is they strike the underside of the toe of the forefoot with the toe of the hind shoe.

The desirable length of the back used to be a controversial subject, with the body of opinion inclining towards a short back as being the stronger structure. In theory this is so, but there are disadvantages. An exaggeratedly short back is uncomfortable to the rider, who will receive much of the thrust of the quarters in the seat. It is less able to absorb concussion and may, therefore, be damaged in one way or another, possibly in the spinal complex, and it can result in a quite unwanted shortening of the thorax. Certainly it limits the stride of the hindlegs and therefore reduces the speed potential.

A back somewhat longer than shorter is now looked upon as being a more desirable feature, that of a mare being acceptably longer than that of a gelding. It will be less susceptible to damage and it allows for greater speed because the hindlegs can be brought further under the body to produce greater propulsion and a longer stride. Length in the back, within reason, is usually accompanied by powerful loins and quarters, the former being as critical to the performance as any other part.

Length in the loin (the area between the saddle and the croup)

(Below and opposite):
a. Good quarters as viewed from the rear. The side of each imaginary square is equal to the length of head in the proportionate horse. The vertical line passes straight upwards from the fetlock through the point of the hock.
b. Weak quarters, 'split up behind'.
c. Cow hocks – a weak structure in terms of performance and usually prone to disease.

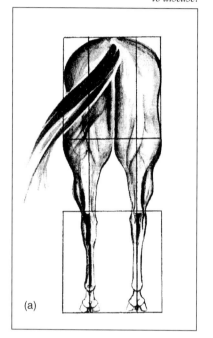

(a)

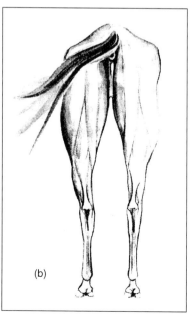

(b)

is not nearly so forgivable. It must be very strong, the muscles being thick, *short* and powerful, for upon the loin depends much of the propulsive force of the quarters. To cover the vital organs it needs to be *broad*. If it is too long there will be a tell-tale hollow space between the pin bone, or angle of the haunch, and the last rib. That is a sure indication of a weak construction (slack) and the opposite of a 'well ribbed up' horse.

The highest part of the quarter is the croup, which in the riding horse should be in line with the withers. Occasionally, however, one comes across a 'goose-rump', a description applied to a high, prominent croup formation. It may appear a little unsightly and give the impression of quarters sloping away into a low-set tail but, in fact, a 'goose-rump' is indicative of good bone development which is advantageous for the attachment of muscle. Horses with this particular conformation are almost invariably good jumpers and, indeed, a 'goose-rump' is often referred to as a 'jumper's bump'.

In the Arab horse, and sometimes in his near relations too, the croup is long and level with the sacrum, the single bone upon which the pelvis rests, being tipped upwards to give the characteristic high tail placement of the breed. In the Thoroughbred horse the sacrum tilts more downwards and the tail is in consequence placed a little lower.

Notably low-set tails, however, and a pronounced slope from the croup, usually accompany quarters which are mean in appearance and are generally weak throughout. Good, powerful quarters are essential in a riding horse that is required to gallop and jump, or to perform an adequate dressage test, and it would be unwise to consider the purchase of a horse that fails in this department.

The quarters are best viewed from the rear. They should look rounded and almost pear-shaped widening into strongly developed *gaskins* or second thighs. A good way to assess the excellence or otherwise of the quarters is to superimpose, if only in the mind, two squares as shown in the accompanying diagram. The side of each square should equal the length of the head. Thereafter a vertical line, drawn upwards from the fetlocks, should pass through the centre of the hocks. Limbs which deviate at all from that line reveal a serious conformational defect resulting in strains and irregularities which may lead to disease in the joints of the hindlegs.

Hips should be level and they must not protrude unduly. When one hip is always carried lower than the other the horse is said to have a 'dropped pin'. This is usually the result of some injury, possibly sustained by the hip being banged against a door post. For the most part it seems to have little or no effect upon the performance, but in some instances there may be unlevelness in the action of the hindlegs.

A bad fault, associated with generally weak quarters, is for the horse to be 'split up behind'. This is a condition in which the juncture of the thighs occurs high up under the tail and is caused by poor development of the second thighs, which provide so much of the power needed for jumping.

Essential to the performance and athletic ability of the horse is the placement of the hindleg in relation to the hip and the positioning and the shape of the hock, the joint which is required to do more work than any other and is subject to a greater variety of strains.

A guide to the hock placement is the chestnut on the inside of the foreleg. In perfection this should be in line with the point of the hock. If that requirement is fulfilled then almost inevitably the second thigh will be long, and because of a short cannon bone the hock will be 'set low' in relation to the ground line.

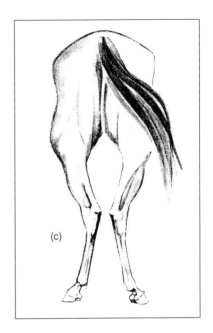
(c)

In perfection a line dropped from the point of the buttock to the ground should touch the point of the hock and coincide with the vertical line formed by the rear of the cannon bone. Translated into performance that means that there should be maximum leverage in the leg components which will result in greater speed and power.

Horses in which the croup is somewhat higher than the withers, a conformation sometimes found in the best Thoroughbred sprinting strains, may also have longer cannons behind, which puts the hock higher than would be acceptable in a riding horse. The arrangement may, indeed, be conducive to speed but it does little for the balance of the horse or the comfort of the rider.

Conversely, many good jumpers and hunters, carry the hocks in advance of the vertical line and the cannon bone is similarly placed. The ability to gallop fast is certainly reduced but the greater degree of articulation in the joints provides a more powerful thrust for jumping and is by no means unsuitable for a dressage horse either.

Hocks and cannons carried well to the rear of the line dropped from the point of the buttock are described, very tellingly, as being 'in the next county'. In this instance, there will be a noticeable lack of propulsive power as a result of a pronounced inability for the hocks to be engaged under the body. Conversely, the hock can be too straight, and with the cannon bone being in advance of the vertical. Both conditions result in uneven wear and subject the limb to greater concussion.

Ideally, for the hock placement to be correct a triangle formed between hip, stifle and seat bone will be even-sided. The diagram shows the variations which occur in the triangle

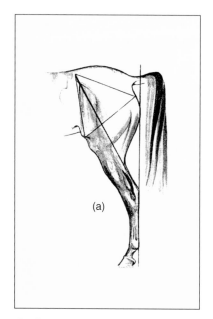

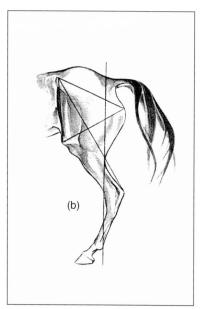

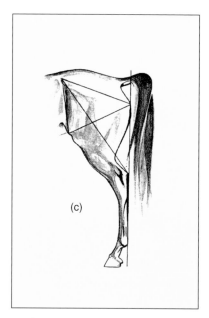

Good quarters. Point of buttock down rear of cannon in line. Length of hip to hock ensures strong propulsive thrust.

Sickle hocks. Sides of triangle unequal.

Hocks too high, cannon over-long.

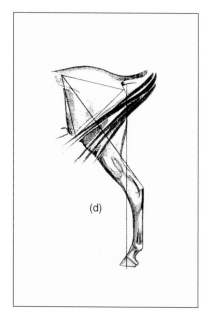

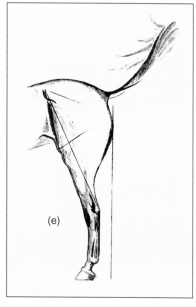

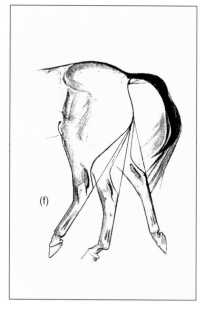

Hocks held too far to rear to the detriment of propulsive effort. (Hocks 'in the next county'.)

Over-straight hocks. Some inequality in sides of triangle.

The ideal for the hock in movement. Straight line from buttock continued along the cannon.

measurements when the hocks are either over-straight or carried too far behind the body.

The principal faults occurring in the hock are when they are over-bent and curved on the front surface, *sickle* hocks; when the points are carried outside the vertical line and the lower limb inside, *bowed* hocks; and then the opposite, *cow* hocks, in which the points almost touch each other. All these conditions predispose the joint to being damaged.

Good hocks are large. Within reason, the larger the hock joint the better, for then the surface area available to absorb concussion will be greater. For all that, it is possible for the joint to be too large, when it will appear lumpy and fleshy and generally lymphatic. Hocks like this will be seen in horses having a high percentage of cart blood. Their effect is to put the whole leg out of balance, the joint itself being limited in its flexion and thus restricting the action.

Finally, as with all joints, the hocks have to be equal in size. Where one is smaller than its partner the cause is likely to be disease or some prior injury which has been sustained. Whatever the cause it is very probable that it will become a source of trouble.

The forelegs are as important as the hindlegs. They are best viewed, initially, from the front making use again of the helpful, imaginary vertical line. Let it commence at the point of the shoulder and pass through the centre of knee and fetlock to the ground. Limbs held or shaped so as to lie outside the vertical

Forelegs. Good – feet straight, knee and fetlock in line;

Turned out toes;

Pigeon toes.

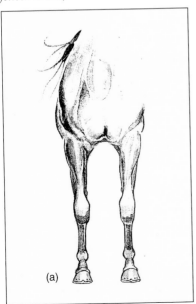

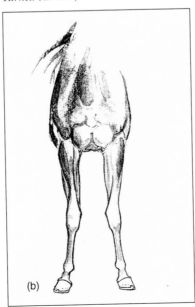

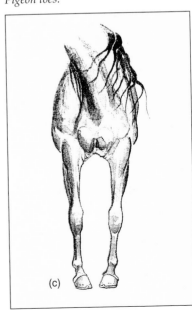

(a)

(b)

(c)

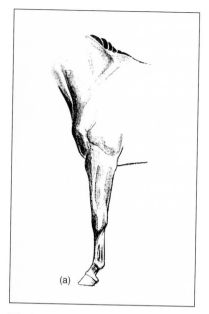

The Lower Limb:
Good, well-muscled with short
cannons;

Tied-in below the knee;

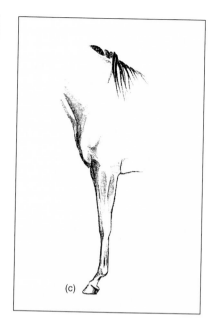

Small knees, light cannons;

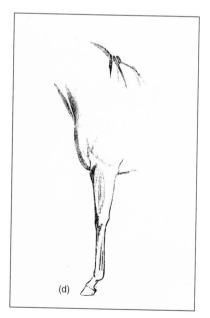

Insufficient bone, cannon too long;

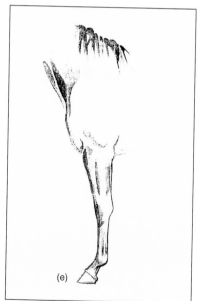

Back at the knee;

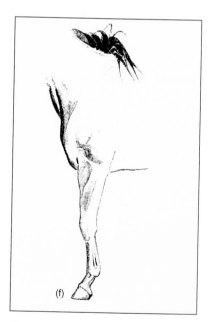

Over at the knee;

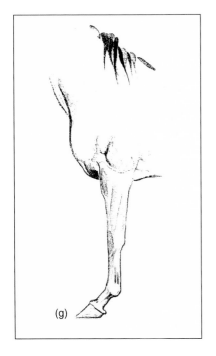

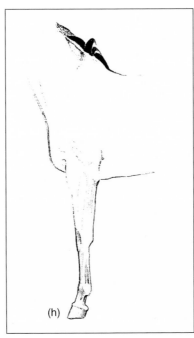

(g)

(h)

(Far Left):
Long pasterns, possibly flat feet.
Foreleg too far under body for generous action;

(Left):
Upright pasterns, boxy feet, straight shoulder.

(Below): a/b/c
The effect of badly conformed forelegs is seen in b and c.

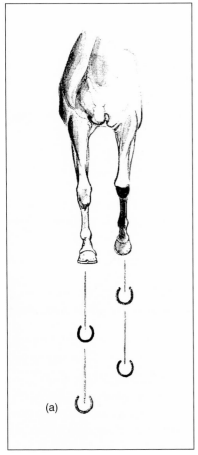

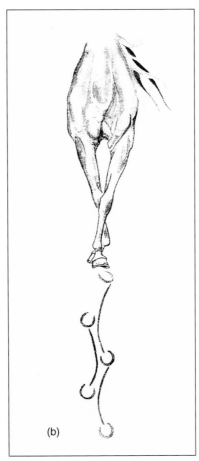

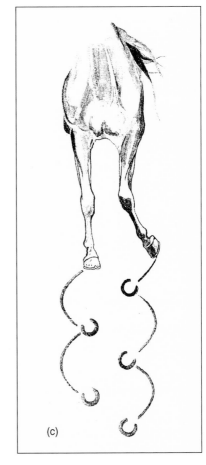

(a)

(b)

(c)

are potentially vulnerable when the horse is put into work.

The next concern is with the elbow. For the action of the foreleg to be unhindered it has to stand clear of the ribs. If it lies hard-up against the latter, making the insertion of a closed fist between it and the body difficult, then it is said to be 'tied-in' and will in consequence restrict the movement of the shoulder. If, because of the length of the humerus, the elbow is set far back the spine will be subjected to greater concussion, as well as the components of the leg and, indeed, the rider, too. A badly placed elbow puts extra strain on the hocks, which have to work harder to compensate for the failing in the forelimbs.

The forearm itself has to be long and very muscular so that the knee is set low on short cannon bones. Like the hock the knee must be large and flat on its surface, not rounded and fleshy. A good knee will have a well-defined pisiform bone and the carpal sheath (a channel) will be broad enough to take the flexor tendon without the latter being pinched. Small, round knees are invariably associated with chronic tendon problems. Once more, the knees, which have to be absolutely straight in relation to the remainder of the leg, must be of equal size and shape.

Knees which are high off the ground are those which are set on *long* cannon bones and the latter have to be regarded as an inherent structural weakness.

Faults in the lower limb which are unforgiveable are when the leg curves inward below the knee. It is sometimes called 'back at the knee' and often also termed a 'calf-knee'. It is a certain source of tendon problems and is of little use in absorbing concussion.

Just as bad, since the construction restricts the passage of the tendons, is a horse which is 'tied-in below the knee', that is when the measurement below the knee is less than that lower down and above the fetlock joint. 'Over at the knee' is when the cannon slopes back below the knee, the latter seeming to be placed in advance of the lower limb. It can be a sign of hard work (witness the nineteenth-century prints of worn-out 'screws' and 'jades') or it is just part of the animal's natural conformation. Whatever the reason it has no inhibiting effects.

Bone, as much-beloved a horsy topic as a 'sloping shoulder', is the measurement round the cannon below the knee. It, and not the height nor build of the horse, governs the ability to carry weight. The more 'bone' the greater will be the horse's capacity to carry weight. Twenty centimetres (8in) will do for most of us, but the 95kg (15-stoners) will need an inch or two more than that.

Actually, of course, when 'bone' is measured we are also measuring the whole structure of ligaments, tendons and tissue which surround the bone. There should, therefore, be no hint of soft puffiness, rather the cannon should feel hard and cool and flat, just as should the fetlock joints. Puffy joints are a fair indication of the amount of mileage covered and how the structure has stood up to the work involved.

The pastern, into which the fetlock runs, is a shock absorber. If it is short and upright it will be less efficient in that respect. If unduly long, the ride will certainly be comfortable but one has to suspect a potential weakness.

Hind pasterns, because of the compensating flexion of the hock, are shorter than the front ones. When the hind pasterns are long it is usually because the hock is unduly straight. The additional length in the pastern reduces the effects of jarring on the hock joints.

Feet are more important than anything else, one supposes, and many experienced horsemen inspect the feet before looking at anything else. If they are at fault there is really no point in looking further. Again, as with joints, you must have feet of equal size and proportion.

Small, 'boxy' feet are prone to disease and best avoided. The horn of the foot has to be strong and thick if there is to be room for the shoe nails. Brittle, broken feet or ones with longitudinal cracks are suspect. Ones with rings round them tell us that the horse has suffered from laminitis.

White feet are thought to be softer than slatey blue ones and they probably are, but there is no reason to turn down a horse on account of a white foot.

Soles of the feet need to be concave (not flat) and they have to be thick enough so as not to be damaged on rough going. Flat, dropped soles are all too easily bruised. The heels on a good foot are deep and open, and the frog, the foot's anti-concussion and anti-slip device, should be large and well-defined.

All four feet should face directly to the front if the action is to be straight and true. Feet which turn out are far worse than those that turn inwards because in movement they are likely to strike into each other.

An inspection of the shoes will tell you a lot about a horse's way of going. If the action is true the wear will be even, if not take note of a hind shoe showing more wear at the toe than its partner, it denotes a less than perfect flexion of the joints on that side.

There are failings in conformation which can be overlooked but if you want a sound, competition horse with a top-level performance potential there are not too many around.

Index